Welcome to a coming war-torn World...

THE FUTURE WAR PROPHECIES

ARAB-ISRAELI WAR
GOG OF MAGOG WAR
WAR IN HEAVEN
ARMAGEDDON

BILL SALUS

Author of the
NOW, NEXT, LAST, FINAL &
MILLENNIUM
Prophecies

but it's only Temporary...
Micah 4:3

The FUTURE WAR Prophecies

First printing August 2023

Copyright © 2023 by Bill Salus. All rights reserved. No part of this book may be used or reproduced in any manner whatsoever without written permission of the publisher, except in the case of brief quotations in articles and reviews.

Publisher: Prophecy Depot Publishing
Customer Service: 714-376-5487
P.O. Box 5612
La Quinta, CA 92248
www.prophecydepotministries.net

ISBN: 978-1-7377901-0-5
Interior by Mark Lambert
Cover by Matthew Salhus
Editing by Karol Bankston
Researchers are Bill Salus, Brad Myers and Ned and Karol Bankston
Typesetting by Mark Lambert

Printed in the United States of America
All Scripture quotations, unless otherwise indicated, are taken from the New King James Version. Copyright © 1982 by Thomas Nelson, Inc. Used by permission. All rights reserved.

Scripture verses marked NASB are taken from the New American Standard Bible, © Copyright 1960, 1962, 1963, 1968, 1971, 1972, 1973, 1975, 1977, 1995 by The Lockman Foundation. Used by permission.

Scripture verses marked ASV are from the American Standard Version of the Bible.
Scripture verses marked RSV are from the Revised Standard Version of the Bible,copyright 1946, 1952, 1971 by the Division of Christian Education of the NationalCouncil of Churches of Christ in the USA.
Used by permission.
Scripture verses marked KJV are from the King James Version of the Bible.

ii

Acknowledgements

Heartfelt thanks to my wife, children, grandchildren and friends who inspired me to write this book. A further debt of gratitude is extended to Ned and Karol Bankston, Bill and Beverly Williams, Ladd Holton, Brad Myers, Mark Lambert and our wonderful Prophecy Depot Ministry Partners and all those who in one way or another, through prayer, encouragement, support, research, or otherwise, genuinely blessed this book.

Table Of Contents

Acknowledgements iii

Introduction x

Chapter 1
Why Bible Prophecy is Important 1
   How Important is Bible Prophecy? 2

Chapter 2
The Role of the Jews in Bible Prophecy 6
   The SEED Prophecies about the Messiah Jesus Christ 8

Chapter 3
The Past War Prophecies 11
   The Exodus War 11
   Gideon's War 15
   The Babylonian Conquest and then The Persian War 17
   World Wars 1 and 2. 21

Chapter 4
The First War of Iran in Elam 25
   Jeremiah's War in Elam 26
   Is There a Coming Nuclear Disaster in Elam? 29
   Is the Disaster Caused by a Major Attack on Iran's Missiles in Elam? 30
   Has Jeremiah 49:34-39 Been Historically Fulfilled? 31

Chapter 5
The War Between Israel and Syria 40
   The Destruction of Damascus. 41

The Desolation of Syrian Cities 43
Text of Jeremiah 49:23-27 43
Summary outline of Jeremiah 49:23-27. 43
The interpretation of Jeremiah 49:23-27 in correlation
with Isaiah 17. 44
Has Isaiah 17 Already Happened?. 45

Chapter 6
Israel's Exceedingly Great Army of the Last Days. 48

Chapter 7
The Proxy War that Shakes Israel. 51

The Glory Waning and Fatness Leaning of Israel 52
(Isaiah 17:4) 52
The Harvesting, Gleaning and Shaking of Israel 53
The Valley of Rephaim, the Uppermost Bough and the
Fruitful Branches 54

Chapter 8
The Arab Response to the Destruction of Damascus 57

The Backlash from the IDF Destruction of Damascus 58
What's Next After the Destruction of Damascus? 60

Chapter 9
Psalm 83: The Final Arab-Israeli War. 61

The Plot of Psalm 83 62
The Confederacy of Psalm 83. 64
The Psalm 83 Confederates 65
The Tents of Edom and the Palestinian Refugees Connection. . . . 65
The Inhabitants of Tyre and Hezbollah Terrorist
Organization Connection. 68
The War of Psalm 83 69

The War Details: Psalm 83:9-12 – the Petition to Empower
the IDF to Victory 70

The End Results: Psalm 83:13-18 – the Recognition that
the LORD is GOD. 72

God's Role in Psalm 83 74

The Psalm 83 Objections 76

Did the War of 1948 Fulfill Psalm 83? 77

Why the 1948 Arab-Israeli War did not fulfill
Psalm 83 78

Why Psalm 83 and Ezekiel 38 are NOT the Same War Prophecy. . 79

Chapter 10
God's Middle East Peace Plan 81

Part One of the Peace Plan 82

The Parties to the Plan 82

The Preparations for the Plan 83

Part Two of the Peace Plan 84

Chapter 11
Israel Defeats the Surrounding Arab Armies 88

The Zechariah 12:1-6 Prophecy. 89

Jerusalem belongs to the Jews. 91

The Isaiah 44:24-28 Prophecy 92

The IDF "shall devour all the surrounding peoples". 94

Divine Military Intervention 95

The IDF Gains Confidence. 96

Chapter 12
The Psalm 83 Peripheral War Prophecies. 99

The IDF vs. the Palestinians 100

The IDF vs. Hamas in Gaza. 102

The IDF vs. Jordan 103
The IDF vs. Northern Jordan 104
The IDF vs. Central Jordan 104
The IDF vs. Saudi Arabia 105
   1. Saudi Arabia Prophecy #1 106
   2. Saudi Arabia Prophecy #2 106
   3. Saudi Arabia Prophecy #3 107
   4. Saudi Arabia Prophecy #4 107
The Two Future Prophecies of Egypt 108
   5. Egypt Prophecy #1: (IDF vs. Egypt) 108
   6. Egypt Prophecy #2: (The Antichrist vs. Egypt) 111

Chapter 13
Ezekiel 38-39, When God Upholds His Holy Name 115

Ezekiel 38-39 Overview 117
God the Victor of Ezekiel 38 121
The Timing of Ezekiel 38-39 125

Chapter 14
The Wars of the Seal Judgments 127

The Wars of the Antichrist as the (White Horseman) 127
First Seal: The Conqueror 127
The World Wars of the (Fiery Red Horseman) 129
The War-torn World of the (Black Horseman) 129
The First Future Holy War of the (Pale Horsemen) 131
The First Holy War Victims are the (Fifth Seal Saints) 133

Chapter 15
The Wars of the Trumpet Judgments 137

The Locust War of Torment of the Fifth Trumpet in
Revelation 9:1-11 138

Locusts or Demonic Beings?	139
Are the Locusts A.I. Drones or Robots?	142
The War of the Sixth Trumpet that kills one-third of mankind in Revelation 9:12-21	144
Woe #2, the Sixth Trumpet Judgment	146
Who are these soldiers? Where do they come from?	148
Are they killing people throughout the world, or only within the Middle East?	151
Are they killing believers or unbelievers, or both?	152

Chapter 16

The War in Heaven	154
The Details of the War in Heaven (Revelation 12:7-12)	154
The Seven Abodes of Satan	155
The Lake of Fire: Satan's Seventh and Final Abode	155
The War in Heaven Happens at the Midpoint of the Tribulation	156
Why the War in Heaven is a Woe Judgment	157
Satan Loses the War and the Divine Debate	159

Chapter 17

The Armageddon Campaign	164
Phase 1: The Fall of Jerusalem and Fleeing of the Faithful Jewish Remnant	165
Phase 2: The Antichrist Invades and Desolates Egypt then Returns to Israel	169
Phase 3: The LORD Strikes the Antichrist's Throne and Shuts Down his Global System (The Fifth Bowl Judgment)	172
Phase 4: The Assembling of the Antichrist's Allied Armies at Armageddon	175
The Valley of Jezreel vs. The Valley of Hamon Gog	176
The War Strategy of the Antichrist and the Armageddonites	177

    The Seventh Bowl Judgment 180

    Phase 5: The Deployment of some of the Armageddonites
to Bozrah 182

    Phase 6: The National Regeneration of Israel 184

    Pinpointing Petra as the Place of Refuge for the Remnant 185

Chapter 18
The Second Coming of Christ and the Armageddon Campaign . . 190

    Phase 7: The Second Coming of Jesus Christ 190

    Phase 8: The Battle at Bozrah between Christ and the
Armageddonites. 191

    Phase 9: The Assembling of the Armies of Christ from Heaven . . 192

    Phase 10: The Battle in the Valley of Jehoshaphat 194

    Phase 11: The Victory Ascent Up the Mount of Olives and
Return of the Jewish Remnant 196

Chapter 19
The Second War of Magog 203

    Comparing the Two Magog Invasions 206

Appendices 209

Appendix 1: 209
Why the Destruction of Damascus is a Future War Prophecy . . . 209

Appendix 2: 221
Why Psalm 83 is a Prayer and a Future War Prophecy 221

Psalm 83 as a Future War Prophecy 225

Endnotes 230

Introduction

Welcome to The FUTURE WAR PROPHECIES. This book introduces you to, and informs you about, the biblical wars predicted to happen in the END TIMES. As the Table of Contents illustrates, there are many globally impacting battles forthcoming.

The Bible is the only book ever written that claims the exclusive ability to foretell the future, and the impending wars within it. In fact, the passages below were included within the Holy Scriptures long ago to challenge people throughout the ages. They invite mankind to align history with biblical prophecy to confirm that the GOD of the BIBLE is the only ONE TRUE GOD!

"Remember the former things of old, For I *am* God, and *there is* no other; *I am* God, and *there is* none like Me, Declaring the end from the beginning, And from ancient times *things* that are not *yet* done, Saying, 'My counsel shall stand, And I will do all My pleasure,'"
(Isaiah 46:9-10)

"I *am* the Lord, that *is* My name; And My glory I will not give to another, Nor My praise to carved images. Behold, the former things have come to pass, And new things I declare; Before they spring forth I tell you of them."
(Isaiah 42:8-9)

Isaiah the prophet proclaims that the God of the Bible, is the only divine being in the universe that can predict the future with 100% accuracy. Thus, Bible prophecy is GOD'S sure way of letting humankind know that HE's the REAL DEAL!

The Apostle Peter sums it up below. He says that Bible prophecy is "*completely reliable*" and extremely important "*to pay attention to.*"

> "We also have the prophetic message as something completely reliable, and you will do well to pay attention to it, as to a light shining in a dark place, until the day dawns and the morning star rises in your hearts."
> (2 Peter 1:19, NIV)

The content of this book is based upon the reliability of God's clear commitment to tell what the future holds. The prophetic passages will often be included, so that the reader doesn't rely exclusively on the author's interpretations.

Some of the FUTURE WARS will appear as though they are presently stage-setting in the news and that's because they probably are. However, this book will avoid attempts at "*newspaper exegesis.*" Exegesis is the critical explanation or interpretation of a text. Traditionally, the term was used primarily for work with sacred religious texts like the Bible.

In other words, this book will not draw conclusions based upon current events. It will prioritize the biblical narratives and prophetic perspectives. However, if newsworthy events find a possible prophetic correlation, they won't be ignored. So, have your Bibles and news sources open together, but remember the news doesn't predict the future, but the Bible does.

The FUTURE WAR PROPHECIES book will in most cases identify the following:

- The war prophecy and its specific details,
- The potential timing of the war prophecy's fulfillment,
- Whether it's a God-ordained or man-driven conflict.

It's important to note that there have been past wars that were orchestrated by the Lord and used to accomplish His greater purposes for mankind. Some of these will be presented in the chapter entitled, "*The Past War Prophecies.*" Like these past war prophecies, there will be some powerful FUTURE WAR prophecies that are also ordained by the Lord, such as the invasion described in Ezekiel 38 and 39.

This war will be explained later in this book, but a few key parts of the prophecy are identified below to demonstrate how the Lord can set forth a war into motion and use it for His purposes.

- In Ezekiel 38:4 we find this clear clue as the Lord speaks to the leader of the Ezekiel 38 invasion, "*I will turn you around, put hooks into your jaws, and lead you out.*"
- In Ezekiel 38:16 the invading leader is told, "*in the latter days that I will bring you against My land, so that the nations may know Me.*"

Although there have been, and will still be, major wars that are of the Lord's doing, it's important to note that God will ultimately bring a cessation to all wars.

> "Come, behold the works of the Lord, Who has made desolations in the earth. He makes wars cease to the end of the earth; He breaks the bow and cuts the spear in two; He burns the chariot in the fire. Be still, and know that I am God; I will be exalted among the nations, I will be exalted in the earth!"
> (Psalm 46:8-10)

In the MILLENNIUM, which is the Messianic Age that exists after the "*desolations of the earth*" have occurred, wars will "*cease to the end of the earth.*" During that period, Jesus Christ the Messiah, will restore the planet and reign over it from His throne in Jerusalem.

Isaiah 9:6-7 informs that the global "*government will be upon His shoulder… And His name will be called… Prince of Peace…* Moreover, "*of the increase of His government and peace There will be no end.*" At that time, mankind won't even have military academies or form national armies, rather they won't even learn "*war anymore.*"

"He (*Jesus Christ*) shall judge between the nations, And rebuke many people; They shall beat their swords into plowshares, And their spears into pruning hooks; Nation shall not lift up sword against nation, Neither shall they learn war anymore."
(Isaiah 2:4; emphasis added)

1

Why Bible Prophecy is Important

This opening chapter will explain what Bible prophecy is and why it's critically important for everyone to learn. It was actually a prophecy that saved humankind from extinction.

As the story is told in Genesis 6:13-22, Noah was given a prophecy that heavy rains were forthcoming. These waters were destined to flood the earth and all peoples and animals alive at the time would drown. At the time the prophecy was issued, Noah was given a means for survival. He was instructed to build an ark that measured approximately five hundred feet long. Considering that the length of a typical football field is one-hundred yards, which is only three hundred feet, this was an enormous undertaking.

Noah built the Ark and according to Genesis 7:7, he and his wife and their three sons and three daughters-in-law were the only people that entered it. Genesis 7:17-23 informs that the flood lasted forty days and that Noah and his family were the only humans to survive.

Genesis 9:1 says, " *So God blessed Noah and his sons, and said to them: "Be fruitful and multiply, and fill the earth."*" Genesis 10 gives the identities of the ancient nations that descended from Noah's loins. Several millennia later we all were born through these ancestors.

This historical account provides a perfect example of why Bible prophecy is important. If Noah had not foreknown about the flood and made the necessary preparations to survive it, you and I wouldn't exist!

How Important is Bible Prophecy?

According to "The Encyclopedia of Biblical Prophecy" by J. Barton Payne, there are 1,239 prophecies in the Old Testament and 578 prophecies in the New Testament for a total of 1,817. These prophecies are contained in 8,352 of the Bible's verses. Since there are 31,124 verses in the Bible, the 8,352 verses that contain prophecy constitute 26.8% of the Bible's volume.[1]

Some higher estimates suggest that about one-third, approximately 10,000 verses, are devoted to prophecy. With so many passages of prophecy penned on the holy parchments, obviously the God of the Bible considers this topic to be deemed as important. Here's why.

Bible prophecy is invaluable predictive information outsourced from a loving God with 100% accuracy that is intended to:

- Authenticate the sovereignty of God,
- Equip the followers of God for the days in which they live,
- Spare lives,
- Save souls.

Authenticate the sovereignty of God – Isaiah 46:9-10, which was quoted in the introduction, declares that only God can predict the future with 100% accuracy. The Lord's ability to declare the end from the beginning is one of His signature trademarks that sets Him apart from all of the false gods. When an ancient biblical prediction finds a future fulfillment, the Lord can justifiably say, "*I told you in advance.*"

Equip the followers of God for the days in which they live – The Lord wants to inform us of the future because He wants to equip us for the pitfalls that await us. To equip someone is to prepare them for a particular activity or problem. It also means to provide them with necessary materials or supplies that they need to deal with that activity or problem.[2]

Spare lives – The Lord informs us of the future to protect us. God wishes that none would perish, but that all would have abundant life on the earth and eternal life afterward. Below are a few passages that support this statement.

> "For I know the thoughts that I think toward
> you, says the Lord, thoughts of peace and
> not of evil, to give you a future and a hope."
> (Jeremiah 29:11)

> "For God so loved the world that He gave His only
> begotten Son, (*Jesus Christ*), that whoever believes in
> Him should not perish but have everlasting life."
> (John 3:16; emphasis added)

> "I, (*Jesus Christ*), have come that they may have life, and
> that they may have *it* more abundantly."
> (John 10:10b; emphasis added)

> "And now I, (*Jesus Christ*). have told you before it comes,
> that when it does come to pass, you may believe."
> (John 14:29; emphasis added)

Noah's story is a prime example of how prophecy can spare lives. Another prime example is inscribed in Genesis chapter 41 dealing with Joseph. He was given advance warning by God that Egypt was going to experience a devastating famine.

> "Indeed seven years of great plenty will come throughout
> all the land of Egypt; but after them seven years of
> famine will arise, and all the plenty will be forgotten in
> the land of Egypt; and the famine will deplete the land."
> (Gen. 41:29-30)

Genesis 41:47-49 informs that Joseph wisely gathered and stored up sufficient supplies during the seven years of great plenty for the Egyptians to survive the seven years of severe famine.

Save souls – The fact that the Lord shares, rather than keeps secret, His foreknowledge of the future through biblical prophecies, can make someone grow fond of Him. I did! I became a believer through learning about Bible prophecies.

This happened in 1990 while I was attending a Bible study on the book of Revelation that was taught by the late Dr. Chuck Missler, (May 28, 1934 – May 1, 2018). His lessons incorporated many past fulfilled biblical prophecies. I researched the historical accounts and discovered that they aligned perfectly with their related prophecies. This impressed me and increased my yearning to know the one and only God Who could accurately foretell the future.

Revelation 19:10 says, "*Worship God! For the testimony of Jesus is the spirit of prophecy.*" Bible prophecy can and has led people to the Lord because it testifies of Jesus Christ, Who is the exclusive means of salvation. Alluding to the name of Jesus Christ, Acts 4:12 says, "*Nor is there salvation in any other, for there is no other name under heaven given among men by which we must be saved.*"

Prophecy can be preached alongside the gospel as an evangelical tool.

> "All Scripture (*including the Bible prophecies*) *is* given by inspiration of God, and *is* profitable for doctrine, for reproof, for correction, for instruction in righteousness, that the man of God may be complete, thoroughly equipped for every good work."
> (2 Timothy 3:16-17; emphasis added)

Conclusion

The prophetic "proof is in the pudding," to coin an old adage, is that the Bible is packed with predictive information, which means that at least the Lord considers prophecy to be important. But why would God be enamored with His ability to foretell the future? Is the Lord trying to impress Himself with this exclusive capability? I hardly think so.

The Lord's ability to know the future evidences that He is not someone with too much time on His hands, but He holds all time in His hands. Moreover, God does not give us prophecy to impress us, but rather to inform us. This is because He cares for us. When the Lord included prophecies with the Bible, He wasn't SHOWING OFF, He was SHOWING UP in a unique and undeniable way.

Bible prophecy is the Lord's way of letting us know how much He loves us.

The Role of the Jews in Bible Prophecy

In Deuteronomy 32:10 and Zechariah 2:8, the LORD alludes to the Jewish people as the *"apple of His eye."* In multiple verses, such as Ezekiel 36:12 and 38:14 the Jews are called, "My people Israel." There's a reason for these terms of endearment and this chapter will briefly explain why.

Possessing a basic awareness of God's special relationship with the Jews will help you to understand why many of the war prophecies in this book center around the Jewish people and the state of Israel.

The Jews are the subject heirs of an unconditional covenant that God made with Abraham about four thousand years ago. The covenant was based upon some important promises that were ultimately intended for the benevolence of humankind. Some of the promises are inscribed in the passage below.

> "I, *(God)*, will make you *(Abraham)*, a great nation; I will bless you And make your name great; And you shall be a blessing. I will bless those who bless you, And I will curse him who curses you; And in you all the families of the earth shall be blessed;"
> (Genesis 12:2-3; emphasis added)

Through God's exclusive efforts, not man's, Abraham would gain a "great" name and father a "great nation." It's interesting that Abraham is a primary patriarchal figure in Judaism, Christianity and Islam. Thus, he has obtained and maintained a great name throughout the ages.

The Hebrew word used for "great" is "*gadol.*" In relationship to its application to the "great nation" promise, it can be interpreted as, a distinguished large magnitude of men in number and importance. This large magnitude of descendants is pointed out in the passage below.

> "Multiplying I will multiply your, (*Abraham*), descendants as the stars of the heaven and as the sand which is on the seashore."
> (Gen. 22:17a; emphasis added)

There has never been this many Jews living in the world, thus this promise is obviously yet to be fulfilled, but it must happen or the LORD becomes a promise breaker. I point out in my book entitled, *The MILLENNIUM Prophecies and the NEW JERUSALEM*, that this particular prophecy will find final fulfillment in the Messianic Age when Jesus Christ reigns over the earth for one thousand years.

This large population pledge is a biological promise, not a spiritual one. Abraham is destined to father a large magnitude of descendants that would come through his loins. These descendant relatives are often alluded to as the "Chosen People."

A large population requires a lot of land to inhabit. For example, China presently hosts about 1.4 billion people that inhabit a country area of about 3.7 million square miles. India's population is about 1.4 billion also and they live on an area of about 1.27 million square miles. Comparatively, Israel presently is only approximately 8.5 thousand square miles, which is about the size of New Jersey.

Not to worry, God promised Abraham that he would inherit a large territory, which is commonly referred to as the Promised Land.

> "On the same day the Lord made a covenant with Abram, saying: "To your descendants I

have given this land, from the river of Egypt
to the great river, the River Euphrates."
(Genesis 15:18)

When the land mass described in this verse above is mapped out it portrays an Israel that is about thirty-six times its current size. The full measure of this land will be appropriated in the Millennium.

The SEED Prophecies about the Messiah Jesus Christ

In Genesis 12:3 Abraham was informed, "*And in you all the families of the earth shall be blessed.*" This finds application through the Seed of Abraham and this is where we discover how God's promises to Abraham are also important to humankind at large. The SEED prophecies deal with the Messiah and carry on through Abraham's descendants as identified in the passages below.

Abraham (the father): "In your SEED all
the nations of the earth shall be blessed,
because you have obeyed My voice."
(Genesis 22:18; emphasis added)

Isaac (the son): "And I will make your descendants
multiply as the stars of heaven; I will give to your
descendants all these lands; and in your SEED all the
nations of the earth shall be blessed."
(Gen. 26:4; emphasis added)

Jacob (the grandson): "Also your descendants
shall be as the dust of the earth; you shall spread
abroad to the west and the east, to the north
and the south; and in you and in your SEED
all the families of the earth shall be blessed."
(Gen. 28:14; emphasis added)

In Genesis 32:28, God renamed Jacob to Israel and Jacob went on to father twelve sons and the Jewish race emerged through the genealogies of these sons. The SEED is Jesus Christ and He came through the lineage of Judah, which was Jacob's fourth son.

Revelation 5:5 identifies Jesus Christ as the *"Lion of the tribe of Judah."*

Conclusion

Before wrapping this chapter up into a nutshell summary, it's important to qualify why all of the above promises rest solely upon God's shoulders. I encourage you to read the entire Genesis 15 chapter. In Genesis 15:2 and 8, Abraham asked God how all of these amazing pledges above would manifest. Genesis 15:9-18 provides the details of how God assured Abraham through an unconditional covenant that He, as the LORD, would take full responsibility for the fulfillment of His promises to Abraham and his descendants.

The point is that the prophecies involving the Jewish people and the state of Israel are about God's exclusive ability to keep His promises contained in the Abrahamic Covenant. In order to ensure through Abraham's SEED, Jesus Christ, that all the families throughout the nations would have the equal opportunity of being blessed, the LORD had to take personal responsibility.

So you see, this is not about the Jews, but about the God of the Jews, Who wants all of the families upon the earth to be blessed. Even though the Jews have often historically been a stiff-necked people, protecting these Chosen People from their own foolish follies and evil enemies is not an option, it's an unconditional obligation of the sovereign God.

Are you and your family being blessed by the SEED of Abraham? Remember that God loves all peoples and He proves this by protecting the Chosen People and the Promised Land of the Abrahamic Covenant. The LORD loves Jews and Gentiles and that's why about two thousand years ago He sent His SEED to the earth to save all souls and bless all families.

> "For God so loved the world that He gave His only begotten Son, that whoever believes in Him should not perish but have everlasting life. For God did not send His Son into the world to condemn the world, but that the world through Him might be saved."
> (John 3:16-17)

Salvation and blessings come through receiving Jesus Christ as your personal Lord and Savior. He is the way.

> "Jesus said to him, "I am the way, the truth, and the life. No one comes to the Father except through Me."
> (John 14:6)

Don't deprive yourself of the blessings intended for you in the Abrahamic Covenant. Jesus Christ the SEED of Abraham can give you eternal life for the future and abundant life in the present. He has risen from the dead and alive to bless you now.

> "The thief does not come except to steal, and to kill, and to destroy. I, (*Jesus Christ*), have come that they may have life, and that they may have *it* more abundantly."
> (John 10:10; emphasis added)

3

The Past War Prophecies

The pages of history are lined with a myriad of devastating war stories. Conflicts have been prompted by holy crusades, evil empires in quest of greedy gain or fights for national survival. The results have produced bloodstained landscapes, humanitarian catastrophes, genocidal attempts, martyrdom and refugee crises just to list a few sad scenarios.

Most historical wars have been initiated and fought by humankind, but there have also been powerful wars involving God. In this book we will call these, "The God Wars," because in every instance the LORD consistently used the specific conflict for His greater good. This chapter will take a look at a few of the God wars of the past and point out how the LORD used the warfare as part of His master plan.

In my explanations of each past God war below I will:

- Start with a title of the war,
- Provide the prophecy or prophecies fulfilled by the war,
- Explain God's role in the war, as to if it was initiated by, fought by or merely foretold by the Lord.

The Exodus War (The title of the war)

The (prophecy fulfilled) by the Exodus War is provided in the passage below.

> "Then He, (*God*), said to Abram: "Know certainly that your, (*Jewish*), descendants will be strangers in, (*Egypt*), a land *that is* not theirs, and will serve them, and they, (*the Egyptians*) will afflict them

> four hundred years. And also the nation, (*of Egypt*), whom they serve I will judge; afterward they, (*the Jews*) shall come out with great possessions."
> (Genesis 15:13-14, NKJV; emphasis added)

About four thousand years ago Abraham, who is affectionately referred to by Jews and Christians as, "Father Abraham," was told by God that his descendants would be in bondage for four hundred years. Now how's that for disturbing news?

Note that the LORD was not punishing Abraham, but caringly informing Abraham from His position of foreknowledge that this would be the case in the future. However, this is a two-part prophecy and the good news is that Abraham's Jewish descendants would not be annihilated, but would come out of this bondage with "*great possessions.*"

In order for this prophecy to find fulfillment, the LORD had to engage in a war with Egypt, the aggressor nation. The LORD did not initiate this conflict, but after warning the Pharoah of Egypt through a series of ten severe supernatural plagues, He was drawn into this conflict. This historic account is inscribed in the biblical book of Exodus, hence the name for this war is aptly called the Exodus War.

The four hundred years of bondage had elapsed and the Jews, who were then referred to as the Hebrews, were growing in number and strength. This demographic population shift greatly concerned Pharoah.

> "But the children of Israel were fruitful and increased abundantly, multiplied and grew exceedingly mighty; and the land (*of Egypt*) was filled with them."
> (Exodus 1:7, NKJV; emphasis added)

> And he, (*Pharoah*), said to his, (*Egyptian*), people, "Look, the people of the children of Israel *are* more and mightier than we; come, let us deal shrewdly with them, lest they multiply, and it happen, in

the event of war, that they also join our enemies
and fight against us, and *so* go up out of the land."
(Exodus 1:9-10, NKJV; emphasis added)

Let's hit pause for a moment. Take note from these above passages that at the tail end of four-hundred years of enslavement, the Jews were in a profitable and multiplying mode. They were primed to leave Egypt and head home to their Promised Land with "*great possessions.*"

Pharoah decided to inflict harsh measures against the Jews. According to Exodus 1:11-14, Pharoah burdened the Jews with hard labor and in Exodus 1:16, he issued an edict to kill all the first-born sons of the Jews.

(What was the role of the LORD in this war)? The Exodus War was not initiated by the LORD, rather according to Exodus 1:9-10 it was started by the Pharoah of Egypt. However this war was foretold by and fought by the LORD. It was foretold in Genesis 15:14 whereby Abraham was informed that God would "*judge*" the nation that enslaved his descendants. That nation was Egypt.

This battle belonged to the LORD. He single-handedly and supernaturally defeated the Egyptian army. Exodus 14:24-31 provides the battle details as follows:

1. The LORD created a pillar cloud that separated the Jewish exiles from the Egyptian army. This cloud created darkness in the Egyptian camp. (Exodus 14:19-20).

2. This canopy of darkness enabled God to enter into the camp of the Egyptian army by stealth. Once inside the camp, God somehow supernaturally removed the lug nuts on the chariot wheels causing them to fall off and making it difficult for them to be driven. When the Egyptians realized this it created an atmosphere of panic within the soldiers.

3. "Now it came to pass, in the morning watch, that the Lord looked down upon the army of the Egyptians through the

pillar of fire and cloud, and He troubled the army of the Egyptians. And He took off their chariot wheels, so that they drove them with difficulty; and the Egyptians said, "Let us flee from the face of Israel, for the Lord fights for them against the Egyptians."" (Exodus 14:24-25).

Discovering the wagons without wheels should have dissuaded Pharoah and his army from advancing further. It's important to note that the Egyptian cavalry with its hundreds of chariots was classified as the finest in the known world. By supernaturally dislodging their wheels the Egyptians were shocked and said, *"Let us flee from the face of Israel, for the Lord fights for them against the Egyptians."*

This strategic act of God appears to have been a compassionate, but final warning to Pharoah and his army to stand down. However, the Egyptians should have fled and hopefully some did, but according to Exodus 14:26, the Egyptian army pursued the Jewish exiles into the Red Sea, which the LORD had previously parted for their safe passage on dry ground.

> "So the children of Israel went into the midst of the sea on the dry *ground,* and the waters *were* a wall to them on their right hand and on their left. And the Egyptians pursued and went after them into the midst of the sea, all Pharaoh's horses, his chariots, and his horsemen."
> (Exodus 14:22-23)

What a remarkable sight, chariots missing wheels with panic-stricken Egyptian drivers entering into a massive sea pathway that had been miraculously divided. This desperate act of futility caused the demise of Pharoah and his foolish army. Once Pharaoh and his Egyptian army entered the sea, it returned to its full depth.

> "So the Lord overthrew the Egyptians in the midst of the sea. Then the waters returned and covered the chariots, the horsemen, *and* all the

army of Pharaoh that came into the sea after
them. Not so much as one of them remained."
(Exodus 14:27c-28)

With the defeat of the Egyptians and the rescue of the Jewish refugees, the Lord fulfilled the prophecy of Genesis 15:13-14.

"So the Lord saved Israel that day out of the hand of
the Egyptians, and Israel saw the Egyptians dead on the
seashore. Thus Israel saw the great work which the Lord
had done in Egypt; so the people feared the Lord, and
believed the Lord and His servant Moses."
(Exodus 14:30-31)

Gideon's War (The title of the war)

The *(prophecy fulfilled)* by Gideon's War is provided in the passage below.

"Then the Lord turned to him, (*Gideon*), and said,
"Go in this might of yours, and you shall save
Israel from the hand of the Midianites. Have I not
sent you?" So he said to Him, "O my Lord, how
can I save Israel? Indeed my clan is the weakest in
Manasseh, and I am the least in my father's house."
And the Lord said to him, "Surely I will be with you,
and you shall defeat the Midianites as one man.""
(Judges 6:14-16, NKJV; emphasis added)

According to Judges 6:1, the Midianites had oppressed the Jews for seven years. As a result the Jews cried out to God for deliverance, and God told Gideon that he would empower him to "*defeat the Midianites as one man.*"

Gideon attempted to muster up his troops, but due to the Lord's scrutiny, which is detailed in Judges chapter 7, only three hundred men qualified as fit soldiers. Gideon's army was vastly outnumbered.

According to Judges 8:10, the Midianite army consisted of one hundred and thirty-five thousand men.

Gideon was informed that he would *defeat the Midianites as one man*, not tens of thousands of men. Thus, three-hundred men was more than enough to wage Gideon's war because as the battle details below will evidence, the LORD planned on covertly engaging in the conflict.

Gideon's battle details are provided in Judges 7:16-22 and outlined below:

1. *The Weapons* – Each of the three hundred soldiers were given these peculiar weapons, a trumpet, a pitcher and a torch to light inside of the pitcher.
2. *The Battle Instructions* – The soldiers were to move to the edge of the Midianite camp with their lit torches and to mimic Gideon's actions. When Gideon blew his trumpet, they were to also blow theirs and then shout, '*The sword of the Lord and of Gideon!*'
3. *The War* – "So Gideon and the hundred men who *were* with him came to the outpost of the camp at the beginning of the middle watch, just as they had posted the watch; and they blew the trumpets and broke the pitchers that *were* in their hands. Then the three companies blew the trumpets and broke the pitchers—they held the torches in their left hands and the trumpets in their right hands for blowing—and they cried, "The sword of the Lord and of Gideon!" And every man stood in his place all around the camp; and the whole, (*Midianite*), army ran and cried out and fled. When the three hundred blew the trumpets, the Lord set every man's sword against his companion throughout the whole camp; and the army fled…" (Judges 7:19-22c; emphasis added)

(What was the role of the LORD in this war)? In Gideon's war, the LORD worked His military magic through the overt actions of Gideon and his troops to defeat the Midianites. Somehow, covertly, the LORD mustered up mass hysteria within the Midianite soldiers and *"set every man's sword against his companion throughout the whole camp; and the army fled."*

According to Judges 8:10, one hundred and twenty thousand Midianite soldiers were killed in Gideon's battle. This war fulfilled the prophecy given to Gideon in Judges 6:14-16 and thereby permanently ended the Midianite oppression of the Jews.

The Babylonian Conquest and then The Persian War (The titles of the wars)

Thus far we have studied two God Wars. There are more in the Old Testament, but these two examples point out that God can win wars overtly, single-handedly and supernaturally, like in the Exodus War, or He can do battle covertly in tandem with the Israeli Defense Forces (IDF), like in Gideon's War. Gideon represented the IDF of his time.

The next two case studies will show how God can work through Gentile empires to wage war and accomplish His purposes. The Babylonian conquest fulfilled a disciplinary judgment by the God of the Jews who were apostate and worshipping idols. The Persian War that followed ended this judgment and restored the Jews back to their homeland and their God.

The *(prophecy fulfilled)* by the Babylonian Conquest is provided in the passages below.

> "Therefore thus says the Lord of hosts: 'Because you, (apostate Jews), have not heard My words, behold, I will send and take all the families of the north,' says the Lord, 'and Nebuchadnezzar the king of Babylon,

> My servant, and will bring them against this land, (of Judah), against its inhabitants and against these nations all around, and will utterly destroy them, and make them an astonishment, a hissing, and perpetual desolations."
> (Jeremiah 25:8-9; emphasis added)

> "And this whole land, (of Judah), shall be a desolation and an astonishment, and these nations shall serve the king of Babylon seventy years."
> (Jer. 25:10; emphasis added)

Jeremiah prophesied that Nebuchadnezzar the king of Babylon would become God's servant to take the Jews captive and make the land of Judah desolate. This dispersion and desolation was determined to last seventy years. Nebuchadnezzar was unaware that his war actions were going to serve God's purpose of disciplining the Jews, but Jeremiah let his Jewish brethren know that this king of Babylon was utilized as a servant of God.

Through a series of three Babylonian sieges between 609-597, 587-586 and 582-581 BC, the Jews went into captivity in Babylon where they remained for seventy years. At the end of the seventy years Babylon was defeated in 539 BC by the Persian War.

The *(prophecies fulfilled)* by the Persian War are identified and commented upon below.

> "'Then it will come to pass, when seventy years are completed, *that* I will punish the king of Babylon and that nation, the land of the Chaldeans, for their iniquity,' says the Lord; 'and I will make it a perpetual desolation.'"
> (Jer. 25:12)

This is a two-part prophecy. Part one addresses the fact that the king of Babylon will deserve punishment for Babylon's iniquity. This judgment coincided with the seventy years of Jewish exile in Babylon. This punishment of Babylon would end the prophesied period of Jewish captivity.

Part two is the making of Babylon into a "perpetual desolation." This is yet a future prophecy that will be fulfilled during the Millennium period according to Isaiah 13:9, 20 and Jeremiah 51:41-43.

The next prophecy explains how God plans to restore the Jews after seventy years of diaspora to their homeland and give them a future and a hope. This prophecy evidences that the seven decades of exile were intended to discipline the Jews and ultimately turn their attention back to God.

> "For thus says the Lord: After seventy years are completed at Babylon, I will visit you and perform My good word toward you, (*Jews*), and cause you to return to this place. For I know the thoughts that I think toward you, says the Lord, thoughts of peace and not of evil, to give you a future and a hope. Then you will call upon Me and go and pray to Me, and I will listen to you."
> (Jer. 29:10-12; emphasis added)

The prophecies below point out that, like God used King Nebuchadnezzar of Babylon as His servant, He also subsequently used King Cyrus the Great of Persia as His shepherd. Over one-hundred years before King Cyrus was born, the prophet Isaiah whose ministry spanned between 740-701 BC, foretold this Persian king's future.

> "Who says of Cyrus, 'He is My shepherd, And he shall perform all My pleasure, Saying to Jerusalem, "You shall be built," And to the temple, "Your foundation shall be laid." '"
> (Isaiah 44:28)

In the next passage, Isaiah continues to provide more crucial details about the part that King Cyrus would play in the grand scheme of God on behalf of the Jews.

> "Thus says the Lord to His anointed, To Cyrus, whose right hand I have held— To subdue nations before him

And loose the armor of kings, To open before him the double doors, So that the gates will not be shut: 'I will go before you And make the crooked places straight; I will break in pieces the gates of bronze And cut the bars of iron. I will give you the treasures of darkness And hidden riches of secret places, That you may know that I, the Lord, Who call you by your name, Am the God of Israel. For Jacob My servant's sake, And Israel My elect, I have even called you by your name; I have named you, though you have not known Me. I am the Lord, and there is no other; There is no God besides Me. I will gird you, though you have not known Me."
(Isaiah 45:1-5)

When Isaiah's prophecies were read to King Cyrus he was astounded and said,

"Thus says Cyrus king of Persia: All the kingdoms of the earth the Lord God of heaven has given me. And He has commanded me to build Him a house, (*the second Jewish Temple*), at Jerusalem which *is* in Judah. Who *is* among you of all His people? May his God be with him, and let him go up to Jerusalem which *is* in Judah, and build the house of the Lord God of Israel (He *is* God), which *is* in Jerusalem. And whoever is left in any place where he dwells, let the men of his place help him with silver and gold, with goods and livestock, besides the freewill offerings for the house of God which *is* in Jerusalem."
(Isaiah 45:2-4; emphasis added)

(What was the role of the LORD in these wars)? The LORD did not fight these two wars, but He foretold of them and likely initiated them in order two accomplish the following purposes. The Babylonian Conquest and the subsequent Persian War accomplished God's master plan for the Jews, first to disperse and discipline the Jews and second, to restore them to their homeland. King Cyrus was used to free the Jews from seventy years of captivity, provide them with great riches and restore them back to their homeland.

Reviewing the prophetic roles played by King Nebuchadnezzar and King Cyrus reminds us of what Daniel the prophet pointed out over 2500 hundred years ago.

> "And He, (the LORD), changes the times and the seasons; He removes kings and raises up kings; He gives wisdom to the wise And knowledge to those who have understanding."
> (Daniel 2:21, NKJV; emphasis added)

The *wisdom to the wise* and *knowledge to those who have understanding*, in the case of these two former kings, was that God raised them both up for His sovereign purposes.

World Wars 1 and 2 (*The titles of the wars*)

Having just established the historical precedent of God using Gentile empires for His purposes, it's time to fast forward to modern history. The LORD used the two World Wars of the Twentieth Century for His greater purposes as well. World War 1 prepared the land of Israel for the restoration of the Jews to their homeland. World War 2 prepared the Jewish people for their return.

The *(prophecies fulfilled)* by these two wars are provided in the passage below.

> "For nation will rise against nation, and kingdom against kingdom. And there will be famines, pestilences, and earthquakes in various places. All these *are* the beginning of sorrows."
> (Matthew 24:8)

This prophecy in Matthew foretells that during the beginning of sorrows period, that world wars would occur, (nation against nation), and they would be accompanied with and / or followed by regional conflicts, (kingdom against kingdom). According to Matthew 24:9, the sorrows period precedes the Seven Year Tribulation Period, which is also known as Daniel's Seventieth Week.

World War 1 fought between July 28, 1914 – November 11, 1918, ended the Ottoman Empires' four centuries of control from between 1517-1917 AD over the Middle East. In the aftermath the following countries were either formed or reinstated:

- Afghanistan in 1919,
- Egypt in 1922,
- Saudi Arabia and Iraq in 1932,
- Iran, formerly Persia, in 1935.

Observe that the nation of Israel was not reinstated in the aftermath of World War 1. It was supposed to have been reestablished according to the Balfour Declaration of 1917, which was subsequently ratified at the San Remo conference in 1920. However the country of Israel never manifested in this period, but clearly the land for the Jewish state became available with the defeat of the Ottoman Empire. Thus, World War 1 prepared the land of Israel for the return of the Jewish people.

World War 2 waged between September 1, 1939 – September 2, 1945, put the Jewish people into a condition of despair as a result of the Holocaust. The prophet Ezekiel foretold of this horrific scenario about 2600 years ago.

> "Then He said to me, "Son of man, these bones are the whole house of Israel. They indeed say, 'Our bones are dry, our hope is lost, and we ourselves are cut off!'"
> (Ezekiel 37:11)

That's the bad news, but the good news for the Jews follows in the very next verse.

> "Therefore prophesy and say to them, 'Thus says the Lord God: "Behold, O My people, I will open your graves and cause you to come up from your graves, and bring you into the land of Israel."
> (Ezekiel 37:12)

God calls the Jews, "O My People," and promises to restore them back to the land of Israel. This happened after World War 2. In the aftermath of this war, the following Mideast nations arose:

- Lebanon in 1943,
- Syria and Jordan in 1946,
- And, last but by far not the least, Israel in 1948.
- Thus, World War 2 prepared the Jewish people for their return to their historic homeland.

(What was the role of the LORD in these wars)? The LORD did not initiate these wars, rather they were started by the warring nations. Nor did He overtly fight in these wars, but covertly, He sovereignly controlled the outcomes of these wars to insure that the Chosen People, (the Jews), survived the Holocaust and were restored to the Promised Land of Israel.

Conclusion

This chapter has established the biblical precedent and prophetic relevance for God Wars. The LORD can supernaturally win a war or empower a people, nation or empire to win a war. However, whatever method of warfare the LORD employs, in every instance the battle is prophesied beforehand and used by God for His greater purposes.

> "Surely the Lord God does nothing, Unless He reveals
> His secret to His servants the prophets."
> (Amos 3:7)

The remainder of this book will reveal that there are many more God Wars forthcoming!

The Future Wars Chapters

The remaining chapters explore the future wars that are predicted to happen in the Bible. These chapters are organized chronologically to reflect the sequential order of wartime events that the author subscribes to. However, some of these epic battles may happen in a different succession.

4

The First War of Iran in Elam

(Jeremiah 49:34-39)

Iran's future is filled with double trouble because it is the subject of dual war prophecies in the end times. This Islamic nation is identified as Elam in Jeremiah 49:34-39 and Persia in Ezekiel 38:5. This chapter will cover the first war of Iran at Elam.

These are two distinctly different prophecies. The modern-day map of Iran below shows the ancient locations of these two separate territories. The territory that was once Elam would include the Southwest Zagros Mountains and the provinces of Bushehr and Khuzestan today, which happens to be the locations of many of Iran's air defense systems, underground missile silos and portable rocket launchers that are capable of launching ballistic missiles.

Interestingly, this would also include the shaded area where the Bushehr nuclear reactor is located on the map. Elam encompasses the shaded area where the Bushehr nuclear reactor is located. A nuclear disaster at this reactor may come into consideration within this prophecy.

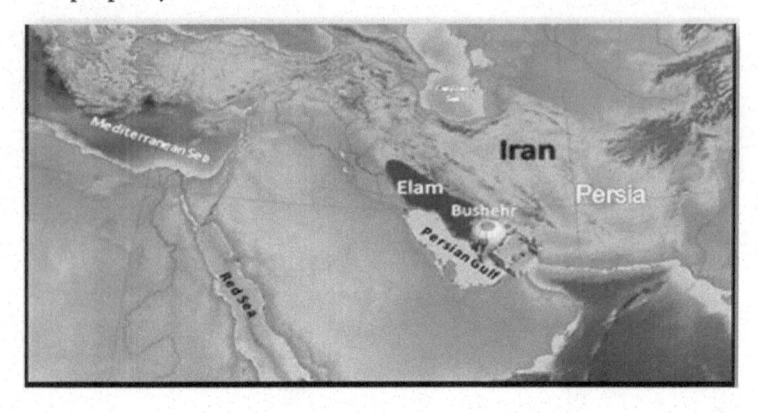

Jeremiah's prophecy concerning Elam is only six verses and is relatively easy to understand. The prophecy appears to be predicting a forthcoming disaster, perhaps a nuclear catastrophe, in the western region of Iran by the Persian Gulf.

Before revealing the details, it's helpful to point out that Iran, as a member nation of the Non-Proliferation Treaty (NPT), has the right to develop a nuclear program, but only for civilian use. However, since the Islamic Revolution in 1979, Iran has been operating in non-compliance with its NPT safeguards agreement, and the status of its nuclear program remains in dispute.

Iranian leadership claims that their nuclear program is being developed exclusively for peaceful purposes and that nuclear weapons are forbidden under Islamic law. Refer to the headline below.

> *"Ayatollah Khamenei says nuclear weapons are 'forbidden under Islamic law'" (The World 5/30/19)*[3]

Herein lies the problem, Israel and a majority of the international community doesn't trust Iran's stated nuclear intentions, and as such, it looks like Jeremiah's war in Elam is about to happen.

Jeremiah's War in Elam

According to the verse below, this war is appointed by the LORD, but appears to be acted out militarily through armies rather than supernaturally by God.

> "For I, (*the LORD*), will cause Elam, (*Western Iran*), to be dismayed before their enemies And before those who seek their life. I will bring DISASTER upon them, My FIERCEANGER,' says the Lord; 'And I will send the sword after them Until I have consumed them."
> (Jer. 49:37, NKJV; emphasis added)

Why DISASTER? Why FIERCE ANGER? The next two scriptures provide the answers. They point out that bad rulers want to launch something lethal somewhere. Jeremiah informs God will prevent this attack from happening.

> "Thus says the Lord of hosts: Behold, I will break the bow of Elam, The foremost of their might." (Jer. 49:35)

> "… And will destroy from there the king and the princes,' says the Lord." (Jer. 49:38b)

We can deduce that the sinister intentions of bad rulers are the provocation of the LORD'S FIERCE ANGER. They plan on unleashing the foremost of their military might upon some enemy. Although we're not specifically told the target, my educated guess in these end times, is that it's the nation of Israel. Jeremiah foretells that these evil leaders of Elam will be eliminated.

God is going to "break the bow of Elam." The broken bow likely alludes to the future destruction of Iran's missile launching capabilities. Poison-tipped or fiery arrows launched by an archer from Elam wouldn't travel the 1300 plus miles to Israel, nor would they do any damage if they did. However, several ballistic missiles tipped with nuclear warheads could wipe Israel off of the map, which is the stated intention of Iran's current leaders. The headlines below point out that Iran plans on wiping the Jewish state off of the map.

> *"Iran general says Tehran aims to wipe Israel off the 'global political map'" (Times of Israel 1/28/19)*[4]

> *"…Khamenei defines Iran's goal of 'wiping out Israel'" (Times of Israel – 11/15/19)*[5]

> *"Iranian commander: We can destroy Israel 'in under 8 minutes'" (Times of Israel – 5/22/16)*

> *"A senior Iranian military commander boasted that the Islamic Republic could "raze the Zionist regime in less than eight minutes."… "Iran in March tested ballistic missiles, including two*

with the words "Israel must be wiped off the earth" emblazoned on them, according to the US and other Western powers."[6]

"Iran says it test-launched new missile with 2,000-km range, capable of hitting Israel" (Times of Israel – 5/25/23)

"Iran's Asef air missile can hit all of Israel" (Asia Time – 3/2/23)

This genocidal mindset of Iran's rulers is a serious problem prophetically because God plans to make His holy name known in the end times through His people Israel.

> "So I, (*the LORD*), will make My holy name known in the midst of My people Israel, and I will not let them profane My holy name anymore. Then the nations shall know that I am the Lord, the Holy One in Israel."
> (Ezekiel 39:7, NKJV; emphasis added)

If Iran possesses nuclear weapons, which would then represent the "*foremost of their might,*" then they could literally wipe Israel off the map and they boast this could happen in eight minutes. Now you see why God has FIERCE ANGER toward Iran, and why He will:

1. "Break the bow of Elam at the foremost of their might,"
2. "Destroy from there the king and the princes of Elam,"
3. "Cause Elam to be dismayed before their enemies, and before those who seek their life,"
4. "Bring DISASTER upon them,"
5. "Send the sword after them Until I have consumed them."

If God doesn't do all of the above and allows a nuclear armed Iran to wipe Israel off of the planet, then He won't be able to let the world know that His name is Holy and He's the "Holy One in Israel."

To "*send the sword after them*" can be interpreted as a biblical typology for causing a military invasion. Jeremiah points out that at the time of the DISASTER Iran will have an array of "*enemies*' and "*those who seek their life.*" At the top of this list of foes is Israel, who takes Iran's existential threats to the Jewish state seriously. Although we are not told who the enemies are specifically, Israel is prepared for a possible conflict with Iran.

"Israel readying for possible Iran conflict, officials say" (ABC News – 11/10/21)[7]

Is There a Coming Nuclear Disaster in Elam?

More details in Jeremiah's prophecy suggest the strong possibility that the DISASTER in Elam causes a nuclear catastrophe. The next verse informs that as a result of the DISASTER, the affected Iranians will be forced to flee worldwide for safety.

> "I will bring against Elam the four winds
> from the four quarters of heaven; I will scatter
> them to the four winds, and there will not
> be a nation where Elam's exiles do not go."
> (Jer. 49:36, NIV)

According to the verse below, the reference to *"the four winds from the four quarters of heaven,"* is a biblical typology that alludes to a dispersion of the refugees.

> "'Come now! Come now! Flee from the land of the
> north,' declares the LORD, 'for I have dispersed you like
> the four winds of heaven,' declares the LORD."
> (Zechariah 2:6, ISV)

Does the DISASTER in Elam include the striking of the Bushehr nuclear reactor? Does this cause nuclear radiation to spread throughout the territory of Elam? Could this cause a humanitarian crisis that forces the exiles of Elam to flee in a worldwide dispersion?

"Gulf countries meet over Iran nuclear radiation fears" (Reuters – 4/14/13)

> *"The earthquake that the Iranian city of Bushehr was subject to has raised a great deal of concern among GCC countries and the international community of a possible damage to the Bushehr nuclear reactor that could causing a radioactive leak..."*[8]

It's important to note that the territory of Elam, being the closest part of Iran to Israel, is a primary location of Iran's underground missile silos and portable rocket launchers. These silos and launchers are capable of hurling numerous ICBMs at Israel in a moment's notice.

Is the Disaster Caused by a Major Attack on Iran's Missiles in Elam?

Will the LORD, who is fiercely angry about what is taking place in the areas of the ancient Elamites, orchestrate events that destroy these ballistic missile launchers stationed there that threaten to destroy Israel from being a nation? If He does this, it would certainly fulfill the *"breaking the bow of Elam."*

It's important to note that Israel, or whoever might attempt to attack Iran's nuclear facilities, will have to face off with the advanced air and missile defense systems and hidden rocket launchers positioned in Elam. Iran is prepared to prevent such an assault and realizes that an enemy attack on nuclear facilities inside its heartland will likely come from the western side of the country, *i.e.* Elam.

In order for any enemy of Iran to reach and destroy the nuclear facilities such as, Fordo, Natanz and Parchin, which are all located east of the Zagros mountains, they will seemingly have to first destroy or at least neutralize the air and missile defense systems in Elam.

In the process of any confrontation, what if Iran's defense systems in Elam are wiped out through major air strikes, or neutralized by an Electro Magnetic Pulse (EMP)? Could that result in the predicted disaster in Elam? Would such a disaster, be it nuclear or something else, in Elam result in a large number of Iranians fleeing into many countries around the world in fulfillment of Jer. 49:36?

Some potential scenarios that could lead to the disaster in Elam and dispersion from Elam are:

1. A strike on the Bushehr reactor, which causes a large radiation crisis that spreads throughout the territory.
2. A massive strike on the missile defense systems, rocket launchers and ballistic missiles inside Elam.
3. An EMP that shuts down the electronic systems and renders the weapons in #2 inoperable. In addition it would make life unbearable for the indigenous population by eliminating the territories' essential electronic needs.
4. A cataclysmic earthquake, which could be caused naturally or by any of the above scenarios. Iran is one of the most seismically active countries in the world, being crossed by several major faults that cover at least 90% of the country. For instance, the Bushehr reactor is built where three tectonic plates converge.

"Iran's Nuclear Plant Sits on Three Tectonic Plates" (Tablet News - 4/9/13)

Has Jeremiah 49:34-39 Been Historically Fulfilled?

Some prophecy teachers believe that Jeremiah's Elam prophecies have been fulfilled historically. The number #1 argument is that it was fulfilled during the reign of Nebuchadnezzar II in the sixth century.

Dr. Mark Hitchcock pastor of Faith Bible Church in Oklahoma did a teaching on his YouTube channel on the prophecy of Elam in Jeremiah 49. In his video "Marking The Times Episode 96 Prophecy of Elam" he says:

"The destruction of Elam took place in the reign of King Nebuchadnezzar."

Dr. Andy Woods the Senior pastor of Sugar Land Bible Church in Texas is a graduate of Dallas Theological Seminary. He also did a teaching on his YouTube channel about the prophecy of Elam in Jeremiah 49. In his video "Middle East Meltdown #26" on August 7, 2022, he says Dr. Mark Hitchcock does the best job he has ever seen on explaining how the prophecies in Jeremiah 49:34-38 actually historically happened. Here are his words:

"Mark Hitchcock wrote a book called Showdown with Iran and in that book there's appendix 1 and appendix 2 and at the very end he does the best job I've ever seen of explaining why those prophecies are not futuristic prophecies but you know actually historically happened. You know for example with the Elam prophecies and I agree that Elam equals Persia which if it was a futuristic prophecy would equal modern day Iran, but it keeps saying Nebuchadnezzar you know over and over again in that section so that's a prophecy that was fulfilled back in the sixth century..."

In his book "Showdown with Iran" Dr. Mark Hitchcock for some unknown reason chose not to provide any historical evidence that Nebuchadnezzar II actually destroyed Elam in the sixth century which immediately resulted in the Elamites being scattered to countries around the world. Why?

Are there any historical sources that show Nebuchadnezzar II in the sixth century destroyed and caused a disaster that resulted in the Elamites being scattered to countries around the world at that time?

In Wikipedia you can find the following information concerning Nebuchadnezzar II and what took place in 597.B.C. with Elam.

"In 597 BC, the Babylonian army departed for the Levant again, but appears to not have engaged in any military activities as they turned back immediately after reaching the Euphrates.

The following year, Nebuchadnezzar marched his army along the Tigris river to do battle with the Elamites, but NO ACTUAL BATTLE HAPPENED as the Elamites retreated out of fear once Nebuchadnezzar was a day's march away."[9]

The editors of Encyclopedia Britannica make available the following historical account of what took place between Nebuchadnezzar and Elam in 596/595.

"After a further brief Syrian campaign in 596/595, Nebuchadnezzar had to act in eastern Babylonia to repel a threatened invasion, probably from Elam (modern southwestern Iran)."[10]

In the Keil and Delitzsch Biblical Commentary on the Old Testament they say:

"Even if Nebuchadnezzar were then occupied in the eastern portion of his kingdom, yet there is nothing at all to prove that he was involved in war with Media or Elam. History says nothing of a war waged by Nebuchadnezzar on Elam, nor does this prophecy furnish any support for such an assumption."[11]

J. A. Thompson in his commentary, "The Book of Jeremiah," on page 33 said that a broken text in the Babylonian Chronicle MAY indicate a CLASH between Nebuchadnezzar and Elam in 596 B.C.

"A broken text in the Babylonian Chronicle may indicate a clash between Nebuchadnezzar and Elam in 596 B.C. to prevent an Elamite advance into Babylonia."[12]

The following source, documents some of the history of Nebuchadnezzar II in one of the historiographical texts from ancient Babylonia in the time frame of about 597. This historical information was discovered in the Babylonian Chronicles. It documents Nebuchadnezzar's encounter with the king of Elam.

"The Chronicle Concerning the Early Years of Nebuchadnezzar II (ABC 5) is one of the historiographical texts from ancient Babylonia ... in 597 BCE..."

Here is a little of what has been found in the Babylonian Chronicle between Nebuchadnezzar II of Babylon and Elam.

"[Obv.15] In the first year of Nebuchadnezzar [604/603] in the month of Simanunote he mustered his army."

"[Rev.16'] In the ninth year [596/595], the month of [...] the king of Akkad and his troops marched along the bank of the Tigris [...]"

"[Rev.20'] the king of Elam was afraid and, panic falling on him, he returned to his own land."

This historical account in the Babylonian Chronicles seems to give credence to the idea that there may not have been an actual battle. In the historical account in the Babylonian Chronicles there was no mention of a destruction of Elam and Nebuchadnezzar's armies did not kill the king of Elam as the biblical text requires in Jeremiah 49.

Jer. 49:36 says that the population will scatter out of Elam into the nations of the world and Jer. 49:38 specifically predicts the kings and princes of Elam will be destroyed. The king not only survived, but rather than scatter away from Elam, he returned back to Elam. These two facts mitigate against the possibility that the Elam prophecy found fulfillment through Nebuchadnezzar II.

Hitchcock and Woods point out that Nebuchadnezzar is mentioned in Jer. 49:28-33 and by association and in keeping within the context, that Nebuchadnezzar was also involved in Jer. 49:34-39 about Elam. They believe this in large part because Jer. 49:28-33 states that the judgment of Kedar and Hazor would be by King Nebuchadnezzar and that did happen historically. Thus, they think King Nebuchadnezzar would also be responsible in the fulfillment of the Elam prophecy. However, they provide no historical proof.

Nebuchadnezzar is mentioned specifically in Jeremiah 34:1, 39:1, 46:2,13,26, 49:28, 50:17 and 51:4, etc., why did the Lord not inspire Jeremiah to put his name in Jeremiah 49:34-39? Did he omit Nebuchadnezzar's name intentionally because this king is not involved in the Elam prophecies.

Moreover, **King Nebuchadnezzar is not identified in any other** of the Jeremiah 49 prophecies of Ammon in Jer. 49:1-6, Edom in Jer. 49:7-22, Damascus, Hamath and Harpad in Jer. 49:23-27 and Elam in Jer. 49:34-39. So, would they connect King Nebuchadnezzar with the fulfillment for these other prophecies, even though he's not associated with any of them?

Another problem for their view is that in 612 BC Babylon destroyed the Assyrian capital of Nineveh and split the Assyrian empire and delivered Elam to Media at that time.[13] This happened about sixteen years before Jeremiah issued his Elam prophecy in 596 BC. They will have to prove when King Nebuchadnezzar conquered Elam after 596 BC, but before he died in 561 BC.

The next relevant question, is "why is God so fiercely angry" as per Jer. 39:37 at the Elamites during the time of Nebuchadnezzar II that he uses this king to destroy Elam? Where is the historical proof of this fierce anger at that time?

Where is the historical evidence that Nebuchadnezzar's armies chased the Elamites with the sword (Jer. 49:37) and killed their king and government officials (Jer. 49:38) in any of the historical accounts found from any source?

Keep in mind that the biblical text in Jeremiah 49:34-38 does not simply say that Elam was defeated. It actually gives many details of what actually happens after the defeat. Should we ignore details in the actual biblical text of end time passages when we come up with our interpretations?

Do highly respected traditional dispensationalists like Dr. Arnold Fruchtenbaum, Dr. Arno Gaebelein, Dr. J. Dwight Pentecost, Dr. Charles Dyer and Dr. John Walvoord agree with Dr. Mark Hitchcock and Dr. Andy Woods that Nebuchadnezzar II fulfilled the prophecies in Jeremiah 49:34-38? Below are some quotes from these respected prophecy experts.

Dr. Arnold Fruchtenbaum writes about Jeremiah 49:34-39 as a future prophecy on page 510 of his book entitled, "The Footsteps of the Messiah." In fact, this is where I first heard about Jeremiah's Elam prophecy. Several years ago at a conference, I asked Arnold if he thought Jeremiah 49:34-38 could have been historically fulfilled, but Jeremiah 49:39 remains unfulfilled.

This partial fulfillment is what some teach. They conclude from Jer. 49:39 that at least this last verse happens in the future because it reads, "But it shall come to pass in the latter days: I will bring back the captives of Elam,' says the Lord." Dr. Fruchtenbaum thought quietly for a moment and then said, "No, it all has to happen in the future at the same time."

Dr. Arno Gaebelein, the author of the Annotated Bible in 1922, believed that Elam's overthrow is foretold in the latter days and he appears unconvinced that the destruction and overthrow of Elam was fulfilled in the sixth century when he notes:

> "*The final prediction is as to Elam. Elam was east of South Babylonia and the lower Tigris, later known as Susians. This*

prophecy was given at the beginning of Zedekiah's reign. Elam became an ally of the Persian kingdom. Here her overthrow is foretold as well as her restoration "in the latter days."[14]

Dr. J. Dwight Pentecost in his classic prophecy book, "*Things To Come*," published in 1958 on page 264 believes in a future fulfillment of Jeremiah 49:34-39 when he wrote the following,

> "*There is a divine program for the Gentile nations that is to come to fulfillment in the tribulation period.... The Judgments upon Nations Adjacent to Israel.... These predictions are set forth in various portions of the Old Testament...Elam (Jer. 49:34-39).*"

Dr. John Walvoord is a well-respected theologian and served as President of Dallas Theological Seminary. He was a professor of systematic theology for 50 years and is considered to be one of the world's top interpreters of end time prophecy. In his very popular book, "*The Bible Knowledge Commentary*" he says,

> "*Though there is some evidence that Nebuchadnezzar defeated the Elamites about 596 B.C., his subjugation at that time did not fulfill this message.*"[15]

Notice that Dr. Walvoord believed Nebuchadnezzar in 596 B.C. at that time did not fulfill the message of Jeremiah 49:34-38. Dr. Charles Dyer echoes nearly the exact same sentiment in the Moody Bible Commentary. Dr. Charles Dyer and Eva Rydelnik on page 1181 state:

> "*Though there is some evidence that Nebuchadnezzar defeated the Elamites about 596 B.C., their subjugation at that time did not fulfill this message.*"

Observe the only difference between the Walvoord and Dyer quotes above is the use of the word "his" vs. "their."

Dr. Andy Woods in his teaching on Elam in his video " Middle East Meltdown #26 on August 7, 2022, actually recommends that people read Dr John Walvoord's excellent book "*Every Prophecy of the Bible*" that was published in 1999. Let's turn to page 151 and see what Dr. Walvoord wrote about Jeremiah 49:34-39 concerning Elam. Dr. Walvoord pens these words:

> "*Jeremiah 49:34-39. The prophecy concerning Elam referred to an area east of Babylon, known today as Iran. The destruction of Elam was described as breaking her bow, for, like Kedar, Elam was noted for archery. The complete destruction of Elam does not seem to have been fulfilled in history and may have its final chapter in the future in connection with the judgements at the second coming of Christ. Elam was promised, however, restoration (v 39).*"

As you can read, Dr. John Walvoord clearly says "the COMPLETE DESTRUCTION OF ELAM DOES NOT SEEM TO HAVE BEEN FULFILLED IN HISTORY..."

Is it possible that Dr. Arnold Fruchtenbaum, Dr. Arno Gaebelein, Dr. J. Dwight Pentecost, Dr. Charles Dyer and Dr. John Walvoord most likely looked at the historical evidence in the sixth century about Nebuchadnezzar II concerning Elam in Jeremiah 49 and concluded without looking at newspaper headlines in their days that the complete destruction of Elam does not seem to have been fulfilled in history?

If the complete destruction of Elam does not seem to have been fulfilled in history, wouldn't this logically mean that the prophecies of Elam in Jeremiah 49:34-38 are going to take place sometime in the future? Who could God be so fiercely angry at in modern-day Iran in our day? Could it be the rogue Islamic regime that wants to wipe Israel off of the map?

Conclusion

The war in Elam is the first in a series of future end times wars whereby the LORD acts upon His FIERCE ANGER. Upcoming chapters will point out that once God begins to execute His fury and vengeance upon His enemies there will be no turning back the clock and globally impacting wars will occur in rapid succession!

Those nations and terrorist populations who stand in the way of God's plans for Israel and benevolent undertakings for mankind are abruptly about to realize that,

> "It is a fearful thing to fall into
> the hands of the living God."
> (Hebrews 10:31)

For more information about Jeremiah's prophecy of Elam, you are encouraged to acquire my book and DVD entitled, *Nuclear Showdown in Iran, Revealing the Ancient Prophecy of Elam*. You will discover:

- That this is a prophecy for the latter years,
- Why Jeremiah 49 (Elam) and Ezekiel 38 (Persia) are different prophecies,
- Why Jeremiah's prophecy of Elam has not found historical fulfillment,
- The good news for Iranians in Jeremiah 49:38-39. Many Iranians are converting to Christianity and encouraging one another with these two verses.
- "I will set My throne in Elam..." (Jer. 49:38a)
- "'But it shall come to pass in the latter days: I will bring back the captives of Elam, says the Lord." (Jer. 49:39) *** Observe, "*in the latter days.*"

5

The War Between Israel and Syria

(Isaiah and Jer. 49:23-27)

The next major Mideast confrontation that could follow the Elam war is fought between Israel and Syria. This battle could occur in tandem with, or as a result of, Jeremiah's war of Elam. Presently, Syria, which borders Israel to the northeast, sits atop a list of Iranian proxies that also includes:

- Hezbollah: located north of Israel in Lebanon and parts of Syria, *[handwritten: 10/23 — Israel warned — we will destroy Damascus]*
- Hamas: positioned southwest of Israel in the Gaza territory,
- Palestinian Islamic Jihad: formed in the Gaza, but also operates in the West Bank,
- Houthis: situated to the south of Israel in Yemen,
- Shiite militias: localized east of Israel in Iraq and Bahrain.

It is highly likely that any disastrous war with Iran will also be waged against these proxies, who have Israel surrounded. Currently, these agents of Iran, along with Iran, are able to launch thousands of missiles into Israel on a daily basis.

"IDF official: Israel expects Hezbollah to fire 2,000 rockets a day in wartime" (Times of Israel – 10/17/21)[16]

"Gaza matches Hezbollah, can fire 1,000 missiles a day: Israel" (Press TV – 5/13/19)[17]

The Gaza headline is alluding to Hamas's capability of bombarding Israel with rockets in a coordinated effort with Hezbollah. At the same time Syria poses a threat to unleash chemical weapons upon the Jewish state. Refer to the headlines below.

"More Than 300 Chemical Attacks Launched During Syrian Civil War, Study Says" (NPR - 2/17/19)[18]

"Israel hit chemical weapons facilities in Syria over past two years" (Reuters – 12/13/21)[19]

In the event of a conflict involving thousands of missiles sent daily, some that could be chemically tipped, Israel's very existence becomes threatened. This appears to be why Israel is plunged into a full-scale war with Syria. The foretellings of this conflict predict dire consequences for both countries. Syria experiences widescale desolation and Israel undergoes a severe shaking. This chapter addresses what happens to Syria, but a subsequent chapter entitled, *"The Proxy War that Shakes Israel,"* will reveal how Israel gets hit hard in this war.

The Destruction of Damascus

The prophecies related to this epic confrontation are found in Isaiah 17 and Jeremiah 49:23-27. Some prophecy teachers such as, Dr. Mark Hitchcock, Dr. Andy Woods and Charles H. Dyer believe that these Damascus prophecies have already been fulfilled in history. However, many others, including myself, teach that these are unfulfilled future prophecies. This list includes Joel Rosenberg, Dr. Arnold Fruchtenbaum, Hal Lindsey, Vernon McGee, Dr. Chuck Missler, Jack Hibbs, Dr. David Reagan, Amir Tsarfati, Tom Hughes, Thomas Ice, Jan Markell and Brandon Holthaus, just to name a few.

If you are under the mindset that the prophecies found in Isaiah 17 and Jeremiah 49:23-27 have been historically fulfilled, then you must read the related appendix entitled. *"Why the Destruction of*

Damascus is a Future War Prophecy." This entire appendix is based upon historical facts and biblical, not newspaper, exegesis.

> "The burden against Damascus. "Behold, Damascus will cease from *being* a city, And it will be a ruinous heap.""
> (Isaiah 17:1)

Isaiah 17:1 predicts that Damascus will be utterly destroyed as a city someday. The literal interpretation of the verse reads that the city will be reduced to a ruinous heap of rubble. Damascus is thought to be one of the oldest continuously inhabited cities in history, dating back over 4,000 years ago to the time of the Hebrew patriarch Abraham. It is the capital city of Syria.

The leveling of this historic city happens overnight.

> "In the evening Israel waits in terror, but by dawn its enemies, (*namely the city of Damascus*), are dead. This is the just reward of those who plunder us, a fitting end for those who (*attempt to*) destroy us, (*the Jewish state*)."
> (Isaiah 17:14, NLT; emphasis added)

The above verse points out that Israel is acting in self-defense. In this prophecy Syria is plundering Israel and attempting to destroy the nation. So the IDF downs Damascus, but not only this major city, but other significant Syrian cities are desolated during this war with Israel.

> "In that day his strong (*Syrian*) cities will be as a forsaken bough And an uppermost branch, Which they left because of the children of Israel; And there will be desolation."
> (Isaiah 17:9, NKJV; emphasis added)

Isaiah foretells that "*in that day,*" alluding to the time period of the Syrian-Israeli war, that other major Syrian cities will be desolated by the "*the children of Israel.*" This is not referring literally to harmless Israeli children, but they represent the powerful IDF of today that possesses nuclear weapons. The NASB translates *"the children of Israel"* in Isaiah 17:9 as the *"sons of Israel."*

> "In that day their strong cities will be like forsaken places in the forest, Or like branches which they abandoned before the sons of Israel; And the land will be a desolation."

These *"sons of Israel"* are the descendants of their patriarch Jacob, who was renamed Israel in Genesis 32:28. The LORD has restored these progenies of Israel back into the historical homeland of their patriarchal fathers and the IDF is destined to defend their nation!

Isaiah 17:9 uses the idioms of *"strong cities"* and *"an uppermost branch,"* which are a biblical typologies intended to represent the major cities of the "uppermost," or northern parts of Syria. Jeremiah 49:23-27 provides more details that helps us to understand what cities are desolated and how devastating this Mideast conflict is.

The Desolation of Syrian Cities

Text of Jeremiah 49:23-27

> "Against Damascus. "Hamath and Arpad, (*Historic Syrian cities*), are shamed, For they have heard bad news. They are fainthearted; *There is* trouble on the sea; (*Possibly the Mediterranean Sea*), It cannot be quiet. Damascus has grown feeble; She turns to flee, And fear has seized *her.* Anguish and sorrows have taken her like a woman in labor. Why is the city of praise, (*Jerusalem*), not deserted, the city of My joy? Therefore her young men, (*civilian casualties*), shall fall in her streets, And all the men of war, (*military casualties*), shall be cut off in that day," says the LORD of hosts. "I will kindle a fire in the wall of Damascus, And it shall consume the palaces of Ben-Hadad, (*Syrian governmental buildings*)." (Emphasis has been added in parenthesis).

Summary outline of Jeremiah 49:23-27

The *italicized* words below are quoted from the verses above.

1. *Bad News* befalls Syria, making it become *fainthearted*.
2. The disturbing news is that there is *trouble on the sea*.
3. *It cannot be quiet*, referring to the *trouble on the sea*. This could be alluding to lethal missiles launched from the Mediterranean Sea on route to Damascus.
4. *"Israel: An 'Underwater' Nuclear Power (Thanks to German Submarines)"* (The National Interest - 5/14/19)[20]
5. *Damascus has grown feeble*; the entire city is shaken, probably from the severe missile strikes.
6. Everyone in Damascus panics and *turns to flee. Fear has seized* the entire city, *like a woman in labor*.
7. There are many civilian casualties as *young men shall fall in* the *streets*.
8. The Syrian army is destroyed as *all the men of war* are *cut off*.
9. *The LORD*, as the perpetrator of the attack, *will kindle a fire* in Damascus and the governmental buildings, referred to as *the palaces of Ben Hadad*, will be destroyed as a result.
10. *"Israel warns (Syrian President) Assad, (we) will bomb palaces if Iran operations continue"* (Jerusalem Post – 6/14/2022; emphasis added)[21]

The interpretation of Jeremiah 49:23-27 in correlation with Isaiah 17

Jeremiah 49:23-27 and Isaiah 17 are likely parallel passages of the same prophecy. Each provides separate details that cooperatively intertwine. It would be comparable to having two separate news reporters covering the same event from different camera angles.

Jeremiah doesn't directly tell us who causes the destruction of Damascus, but Isaiah 17:9 does. Isaiah identifies the IDF, (the sons of Israel), as the cause of the desolation in Damascus and other fortified Syrian cities.

Isaiah informs that strong cities will be forsaken, but apart from Damascus, neglects to specify which ones. Jeremiah provides those details. Jeremiah 49:23 says, *"Hamath and Arpad are shamed."*

Historically, Hamath and Arpad, in addition to Damascus, were among Syria's most notable, (strong), northern cities. Arpad probably represents Aleppo today, which is Syria's most populated city, and Hamath most resembles the cities of Homs and Hama, which rank as Syria's third and fourth occupied cities. Damascus is the second most inhabited Syrian city.

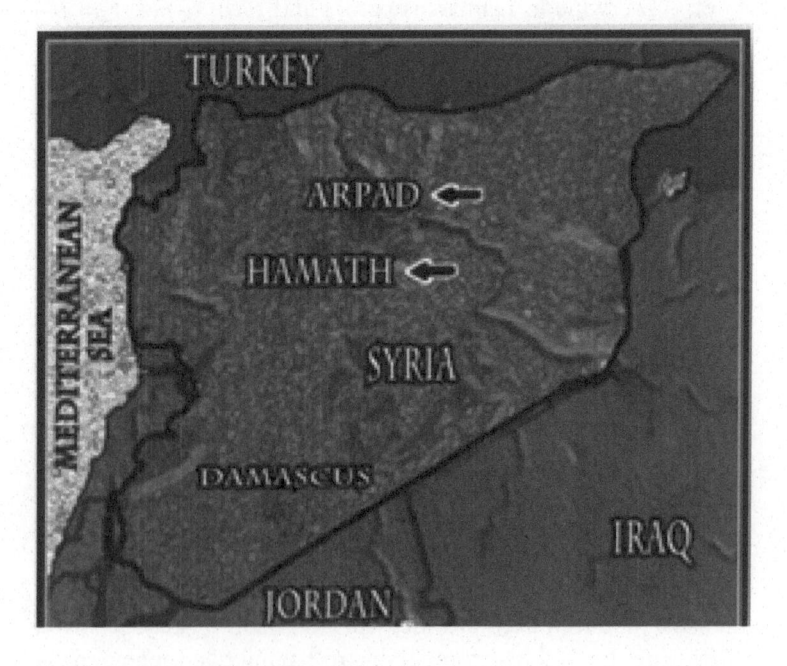

Has Isaiah 17 Already Happened?

Some people wonder if these above prophecies have already found fulfillment in either the Assyrian conquest of Damascus in

732 BC, or amidst the devastation and rubble of the decade-long Syrian Civil War that began in 2011.

Was Damascus destroyed in 732 BC? In addition to the important historical and biblical reasons provided in the appendix entitled, "*Why the Destruction of Damascus is a Future War Prophecy,*" I would argue no and to this question for the following additional reasons.

Isaiah mentions Assyria, Assyrian, or Assyrians at least 41 times in his 66 chapters, but never once mentions any of the above in Isaiah 17. To the contrary, Isaiah 17:9 stated the "sons of Israel," and not the Assyrians or the sons of Assyria, are responsible for this destruction.

Additionally, Jeremiah 49:23-27, which was written more than a century after Isaiah 17, also talks about a burden against Damascus. If Damascus was literally destroyed in 732 B.C. by the Assyrians, this means that it would have had to become restored subsequently for Jeremiah's prophecy to find a future fulfillment. I think it is more logical to read Isaiah 17 and Jeremiah 49:23 -27 in connection with each other to glean more prophetic details about the Syrian-Israeli War.

Does the devastation and rubble that has resulted from the decade-long Syrian Civil War fulfill these Syrian prophecies above? This is not likely because the city damages brought about by this revolution were not inflicted by the IDF. Also, Damascus still exists as of now, which apparently won't be the case much longer.

Conclusion

Presently, Israel and Syria are still enemies of each other. Unlike Egypt and Jordan, who have temporary fragile peace treaties with Israel, Syria does not. Iran continues to supply weapons into Syria that are intended to make its proxies more armed and dangerous. Israel has struck inside of Syria hundreds of times to prevent this flow of weaponry. At some point the IDF will do more than strike weapons depots inside of Syria, but will cause desolation of strong Syrian cities.

"Israel says struck Iranian targets in Syria 200 times in last two years" (Reuters – 9/4/18)[22]

Isaiah 17:14 clearly indicts Syria as an enemy of Israel that will eventually seek to plunder and destroy the Jewish state, and this will become Syria's downfall. The LORD will not allow Iran, Syria or any of the proxies to interfere with His benevolent prophetic plans for Israel.

6

Israel's Exceedingly Great Army of the Last Days

The IDF's destruction of Damascus and desolation of other major Syrian cities identified in the last chapter was prophesied by Isaiah, but this same army is the subject of several other significant wartime prophecies. Syria is only one of the surrounding nations that will be soundly defeated by the IDF. This chapter will introduce you to this end times Mideast superpower army.

> "So I prophesied as He commanded me, and breath came into them, and they lived, and stood upon their feet, an exceedingly great army."
> (Ezekiel 37:10)

About 2600 years ago, the prophet Ezekiel foretold that upon Israel's reestablishment as the Jewish state, the nation would establish *"an exceedingly great army."* The next passage provides some timing clues as to when this would happen.

> "Then He said to me, "Son of man, these bones are the whole house of Israel. They indeed say, 'Our bones are dry, our hope is lost, and we ourselves are cut off!' Therefore prophesy and say to them, 'Thus says the Lord God: "Behold, O My people, I will open your graves and cause you to come up from your graves, and bring you into the land of Israel."
> (Ezekiel 37:11-12)

Clue #1: This prophecy would find an application to *"the whole house of Israel,"* representing the entire Jewish race.

Clue #2: Ezekiel informs that when the world Jewry found themselves in a severely desperate situation they would say, *'Our bones are dry, our hope is lost, and we ourselves are cut off.'* The next clue strongly suggests that this horrific condition occurred as a result of the Nazi Holocaust in WWII, which took place between 1939-1945 A.D.

Clue #3: This prophecy would happen at some point during the worldwide Jewish diaspora, which history confirms lasted 1878 years between 70 A.D. to 1948 A.D. Ezekiel said, that the LORD will *"bring them into the land of Israel,"* which infers that at the time of their extreme helplessness, the Jews would be dispersed into the nations of the world and living outside of their historic homeland.

Thus, Ezekiel 37:11-12 sums up the metric of time that the Jews would be in the diaspora without a homeland, not in years, decades, or centuries, but in their helpless concluding Holocaust condition. In essence, the prophet predicts that when the Jews would be confronted with possible genocidal extermination, their worldwide dispersion would conclude. Ezekiel 37:10 predicts that subsequently, the returning Jews would establish *"an exceedingly great army."*

The formation of the powerful IDF of today has developed out of necessity. From day one, the restored Jewish state of Israel has been forced to fight its surrounding Arab enemies. In the Arab-Israeli War of 1948, Israel was attacked by an Arab confederacy that included Egypt, Syria, Jordan, Iraq, Lebanon, Saudi Arabia and others. Miraculously, Israel was victorious.

In the Six-Day War of 1967, Egypt, Syria and Jordan went to war against Israel once more and again Israel won. In the Yom Kippur War of 1973, Egypt and Syria attacked Israel another time and they dragged Jordan into this war. Again, the IDF defeated their Arab foes. These major Arab-Israeli wars are only a few of the battles that the IDF has been forced to fight and according to biblical prophecies, even more powerful conflicts are forthcoming.

Conclusion

Apparently, God in His foreknowledge, knew that Israel would require a superior military to defend itself from its enemies, Syria being just one of them. Thus, He had Ezekiel foretell of this army for Israel and us in advance. The IDF is presently a great army, but you are about to discover how they become an "EXCEEDINGLY GREAT ARMY!"

In short, the IDF of today exists in fulfillment of Bible prophecies, plural, and the remaining chapters will inform of how well they will perform in their FUTURE WARS of the LAST DAYS!

7

The Proxy War that Shakes Israel

This chapter is an extension of the prior one entitled, "*The War Between Israel and Syria.*" Below is a quote from that chapter.

> "*The foretellings of this conflict, (between Israel and Syria), predict dire consequences for both countries. Syria experiences widescale desolation and Israel undergoes a severe shaking. This chapter addresses what happens to Syria, but a subsequent chapter entitled, "The Proxy War that Shakes Israel," will reveal how Israel gets hit hard in this war.*"

This is the chapter alluded to above. Isaiah 17:4-6 pictures Israel going through a powerful "*shaking*" in the war with Syria that causes the destruction of Damascus. Isaiah's passage states the following.

> "In that day it shall come to pass *That* the glory of Jacob, *(Israel)*, will wane, And the fatness of his, *(the Jewish state)*, flesh grow lean. It shall be as when the harvester gathers the grain, And reaps the heads with his arm; It shall be as he who gathers heads of grain In the Valley of Rephaim, *(in Israel)*. Yet gleaning grapes will be left in it, Like the shaking of an olive tree, Two *or* three olives at the top of the uppermost bough, Four *or* five in its most fruitful branches," Says the Lord God of Israel."
> (Isaiah 17:4-6, NKJV; emphasis added)

These telling verses start with "*In that day,*" which gives us the timeframe when the "glory of" Israel will wane and the "fatness" of the Jewish state will "grow lean." *In that day*, alludes to the time period associated with the destruction of Damascus in Isaiah 17:1.

"The burden against Damascus. "Behold, Damascus will cease from *being* a city, And it will be a ruinous heap."

In this window period of time stated as, *in that day*, the "glory of" Israel will wane and the "fatness" of the Jewish state will "grow lean."

We are also informed as to how this glory to leanness process happens. Isaiah uses agricultural examples of grain harvesting, grape gleaning and olive tree shaking. Moreover, war locations within Israel may be able to be determined by understanding what is meant by the Valley of Rephaim, and the uppermost bough and fruitful branches of an olive tree.

Thus, from these important clues in Isaiah 17:4-6 we can uncover what drives Israel to the point that it feels compelled to destroy the capital city of Syria. The details provided imply that during the conflict the Jewish state comes under a devastating attack, which forces it to desolate not only Damascus, but other major Syrian cities according to Isaiah 17:9 and Jeremiah 49:23.

The Glory Waning and Fatness Leaning of Israel

(Isaiah 17:4)

"*The glory of Jacob will wane.*" Jacob represents Israel according to Genesis 32:28. Prior to the Syrian-Israeli conflict that leads to the obliteration of Damascus, Israel is noted to possess "glory." The use of glory depicts Israel in an exalted condition. It likely describes a prosperous and robust nation of world renown, but as a result of the war, Israel's glory wanes. This suggests that the Jewish state's prominence falls from the heights of its power, prosperity and influence.

"*And the fatness of his flesh* (will) *grow lean.*" The downward slide of Israel's glory leads to the diminishment of its resources. The nation becomes lean, which is a term sometimes associated with a Third

World country that tends to be highly impoverished, economically unstable and economically dependent upon industrialized nations. Thus it appears that Israel enters the conflict as a country blessed by the fatness of its own resources, but in a short order seemingly digresses into a lean nation.

(Caveat: It's important to note that Israel bounces back from this lean condition according to the prophecy in Ezekiel 38, which will be covered in a later chapter within this book).

The Harvesting, Gleaning and Shaking of Israel

"*It shall be as when the harvester gathers the grain.*" The conditions inside Israel at the start of the war appear to be economically sound. The grain harvest, which typically happens in the month of May, is yielding a robust crop. The harvester "*reaps the heads with his arm; It shall be as he who gathers heads of grain.*"

"*Yet gleaning grapes will be left in it.*" However, as the war progresses, the healthy grain harvest scales down to a meager gleanings of grapes in the ensuing grape season. Only gleanings are what's left over after the gatherers have finished collecting the clusters in a robust grape season. The grape harvest in Israel usually occurs in the fall sometime in August to September. Thus, from a healthy grain harvest in May, only table scrap grape gleanings are available around August.

"*Like the shaking of an olive tree.*" From a healthy grain harvest to an essentially non-existent grape season, now Isaiah touches upon the olive tree shaking scenario. The olive picking season in Israel usually follows the grape season and occurs around October and November. The olive tree is a mainstay of Israel's farming economy.

"*There are currently 340,000 dunams of Olive trees planted across Israel, producing over 15,000 tons of oil and over 24,000 tons of edible olives annually. The Olive trees in Israel have been around for centuries if not millennia.*"[23] (A dunam is approximately nine hundred square meters, which is equivalent to about .22 acres).

Isaiah 17:6 says that after the severe shaking caused by the conflict there will only be, "*Two or three olives at the top of the uppermost bough, Four or five in its most fruitful branches.*" So, instead of the annual production of "*15,000 tons of oil and over 24,000 tons of edible olives,*" it seems that as a result of this war there will be no olive harvest at all.

These agricultural scenarios depict how Israel's glory fades and the fatness of the nation grows lean. This is a picture of how the Syrian-Israeli war devastates Israel and provokes the nation to destroy Damascus.

The sequential grain, grape and olive harvest seasons do not necessarily tell us how long the conflict lasts, rather they draw our attention to the dramatic downward digression of events brought about by the war. Israel is not in a position to wage a several months long war of attrition with Syria and the other proxies of Iran, so this conflict will not likely last very long, but the results for all warring factions will be devastating.

The Valley of Rephaim, the Uppermost Bough and the Fruitful Branches

Isaiah appears to be warning that the war is widespread throughout Israel rather than confined to the Golan Heights and general borders between Israel and Syria. The Valley of Rephaim is a valley that descends southwest from Jerusalem to Nahal Sorek, which is one of the largest, most important drainage basins in the Judean Hills.[24]

This suggests that the war extends down as far as Jerusalem. This is probably why Jeremiah 49:25 asks this rhetorical question; "*Why is the city of praise not deserted, the city of My joy?*" The city of praise is Jerusalem. Thus, Jeremiah is asking how come Damascus gets destroyed, but Jerusalem still exists and is not deserted?

The allusions to the "uppermost bough" and the "fruitful branches" of the olive tree in Isaiah 17:6 seemingly identifies northern Israel as the uppermost bough and central Israel as the fruitful branches. If you superimpose the image of an olive tree over a map of Israel, it will locate Haifa as part of the uppermost bough and the fruitful branches could extend into Tel Aviv.

Conclusion

The imageries provided in Isaiah 17:4-6 do not present a good outlook for Israel in its war with Syria. The conflict, which will likely also involve Iran and its proxies, seems to push Israel to the brink of its extinction. This devastating war compels Israel to destroy Damascus and other major Syrian cities. According to the verse below, Damascus gets destroyed overnight.

> "Then behold, at eventide, trouble! *And before the morning, he (Damascus) is no more. This is the portion of those who plunder us, And the lot of those who rob us."*
> (Isaiah 17:14; emphasis added)

This verse uses the masculine pronoun "he" to refer to Damascus. Isaiah declares that one night you will see Damascus, but by the morning the city will no longer exist. Moreover, we are told that, "*this is the portion of those who plunder us, And the lot of those who rob us.*" The plundering and robbing by Syria are the root causes of why the "glory of" Israel will wane and the "fatness" of the Jewish state will "grow lean" as per Isaiah 17:14.

The plundering and robbing that occurs suggests that the Jewish state is being invaded, not only by missiles from the air, but also by boots on the ground. Air strikes destroy plunder and booty, but foot soldiers capture these things. The picture portrayed is a full-scale war whereby Jewish cities and neighborhoods are being attacked, plundered and robbed by the Syrian army and their allies.

Therefore, we discover that Israel is not the aggressor in this conflict, but they are forced to act aggressively to defend the nation. In order to fight off an existential threat from Syria, and probably a coalition of Iran and its proxies, the Jewish state resorts to destroying Damascus overnight.

When this happens, it can be expected that this will cause a major uproar within the neighboring Arab states and probably the entire Muslim world. This war scenario could then initiate the Psalm 83 prophecy, which is the subject of the next chapter.

I'll close with a few headlines that illustrate how Hezbollah has integrated its operation into Syria alongside of terror cells that are proxies of Iran.

> *"Iran Entangled: Iran and Hezbollah's Support to Proxies Operating in Syria" (West Point – 4/21/22)*
>
> *"Hezbollah-backed terrorists form 'dozens of cells' on Syrian border" (JNS - 2/27/23)*
>
> *"Israel drops flyers over southern Syria warning against cooperating with Hezbollah" (AA – 5/17/23)*
>
> *"Israel confronted 'Hezbollah 2' in Syria, but what's its end goal? – analysis" (Jerusalem Post – 12/1/22)*

8

The Arab Response to the Destruction of Damascus

It's helpful to segue into the upcoming chapters by way of review. Up to this point in the book:

1. Iran has been involved in an epic war, probably nuclear, with Israel in fulfillment of the "latter days" prophecy of Elam in Jeremiah 49:34-39.
2. This war in Iran (Elam) has provoked a harsh retaliation by Iran and its proxies against Israel.
3. In order to fend off an existential threat to the Jewish state, the IDF has destroyed the city of Damascus. This happens overnight and probably via the use of a strategic nuclear weapon in fulfillment of Isaiah 17:1,9,14.
4. This fierce fighting with Iran and its proxies has caused Israel's glory and prominence to suffer and has:
    a. Reduced Israel from a fat and healthy nation to a lean one,
    b. Taken a harsh toll on some Israeli cities,
    c. Become excessively taxing upon the IDF,
    d. Probably brought about many Israeli civilian casualties. (See the related headline below).

"The IDF drills for a devastating war on home soil and away"

"Thousands of troops, and hundreds of aircraft and navy vessels all trained together in going to war against Israel's enemies, on all fronts and in all dimensions, including a strike in Iran… The Israeli army expects the home front to be bombarded with 1,500 rockets a day until the last day of the war. The attacks would wreck the country, with dozens of buildings and sites destroyed and hundreds killed and wounded." (Jerusalem Post – June 4, 2022)[25]

The Backlash from the IDF Destruction of Damascus

With this backdrop in review, it's time to ponder what the backlash from the destruction of the world's oldest continuously inhabited city, which happens to be an Arab capital city, might be. It's predictable that the overnight desolation of Damascus by the IDF will not bode well with the neighboring Arab states nor the terrorist organizations within those nations, like Hezbollah, Hamas and the Palestinian Islamic Jihad.

It won't matter much to most Middle Eastern Arabs that the IDF was fending off an existential threat, because the Arab countries are not fond of a Jewish state on their borders. If Israel got wiped off the map, most of these Arabs would revel in Israel's defeat. These Arab states all voted against the creation of the Jewish state at the United Nations in the 1947 Resolution 181. (Read the quote from Israel's Ministry of Foreign Affairs below).

"Resolution 181 was emphatically rejected by the local Arab population and the Arab States. Denying the Jewish people's right to a state of their own, the Arab countries openly declared their intention of preventing the creation of the Jewish State by all means."[26]

Moreover, the local Arab Palestinian population and all of these Arab countries went to war against Israel in 1948. This is when the Palestinian refugee crisis began because Israel won that war and many of the local Arabs were displaced. Then there were more unsuccessful Arab wars against Israel in 1967 and 1973.

The point is that the nations of Jordan, Saudi Arabia, Egypt, Iraq and Lebanon will likely:

1. Be extremely upset that an Arab capital city, with such a rich history as Damascus, has been destroyed by the Jews.
2. Feel threatened that their own capital cities of Amman (Jordan), Cairo (Egypt), Riyadh (Saudi Arabia), Beirut (Lebanon) and Baghdad (Iraq) could become the next IDF targets.
3. Be cognizant of the fact that Israel's become very war-weary and thus vulnerable to attack as a result of the war with Iran and its proxies.

Even though Egypt and Jordan presently maintain fragile peace treaties with Israel these pacts will prove to be paper thin in light of the three points just listed. Moreover, this and upcoming chapters will reveal that Egypt and Jordan engage again in a future war against Israel according to Bible prophecy.

In light of all the above, it's safe to suggest that the Arab states will confederate again like they did in 1948 to seize the opportunity to strike Israel at its point of weakness and to avoid becoming the IDF's next nuclear victim. These Arabs nations and terrorist organizations will likely be extremely upset with the Jews and incredibly nervous about the futures of their homelands and capital cities.

What's Next After the Destruction of Damascus?

Now it's time to see if the Bible predicts a climactic concluding Arab-Israeli war. The answer is YES and it's described in Psalm 83 and many other related peripheral prophecies. The ancient foretelling detailed in Psalm 83, which is the subject of the next chapter, informs that the aforementioned Arab states, which share common borders with Israel, will someday confederate to wage a final war with Israel. The destruction of Damascus could be the catalyst to the Psalm 83 war that:

1. Concludes the Arab-Israeli conflict and,
2. Finally ends the historic Arab hatred of the Jews that has existed since time immemorial!

9

Psalm 83: The Final Arab-Israeli War

Psalm 83 was written about three thousand years ago by Asaph who authored a total of twelve Psalms including Psalm 50 and Psalms 73-83. According to 2 Chronicles 29:30 and 1 Chronicles 25:2, Asaph is identified as a prophet. In fact, his prophecy in Psalm 78 predicted that the Messiah would speak in parables, which was fulfilled by Jesus Christ at His First Coming. Read the related prophetic passages below.

> "My people, hear my teaching; listen to the words of my mouth. I will open my mouth with a parable; I will utter hidden things, things from of old—"
> (Psalm 78:1-2, NIV)

> "Jesus spoke all these things to the crowd in parables; he did not say anything to them without using a parable. So was fulfilled what was spoken through the prophet (*Asaph*): I will open my mouth in parables, I will utter things hidden since the creation of the world."
> (Matthew 13:34-35, NIV; emphasis added)

In Psalm 83 Asaph foretells of the final conflict between the Arabs and the Jews and he beseeches the LORD to empower the Israeli Defense Forces to win a decisive victory. As we take a close look at this prophetic Psalm, we will discover that when it finds final fulfillment, Israel wins the war and the IDF emerges as an exceedingly great army, but on the flip side, the Arab armies are soundly defeated and their slain soldiers are many. Their dead corpses rot throughout the Middle East. Psalm 83:10 points out that these Arab troops become as *"refuse on the earth."*

Current political attempts to resolve the Palestinian and Arab conflict with Israel diplomatically will fail. They are merely prolonging the inevitable, which is the devastating Mideast war described in Psalm 83 and its numerous related prophecies that deal with the Israeli Defense Forces fighting and defeating the Psalm 83 confederates.

The Islamic Arabs are worshipping the wrong god and believe that their Allah will help them wipe Israel off of the map in favor of another Arab state called Palestine. This is erroneous thinking and just the opposite will happen. Jehovah, the one true God will empower the IDF and reduce Allah to nothing in the process. The Psalm ends with this declaration.

> "That they, (*the Arabs*), may know that You, (*Jehovah, not Allah*), whose name alone *is* the Lord, *Are* the Most High over all the earth."
> (Psalm 83:18; emphasis added)

You are about to learn about the foretold war that changes the spiritual, geo-political and territorial dynamics of the Mideast forever and turns this verse above into reality.

The Plot of Psalm 83

> "Do not keep silent, O God! Do not hold Your peace, And do not be still, O God! For behold, Your enemies make a tumult; And those who hate You have lifted up their head. They have taken crafty counsel against Your people, And consulted together against Your sheltered ones. They have said, "**Come, and let us cut them off from being a nation, That the name of Israel may be remembered no more.**" For they have consulted together with one consent; They form a confederacy against You."
> (Psalm 83:1-5; emphasis added)

> "Who said, "Let us take for ourselves
> The pastures of God for a possession.""
> (Psalm 83:12)

This passage in Psalm 83 points out that a confederacy forms and devises a devious plot to wipe the nation of Israel off of the map and the pages of history. Their underlying motive is to take possession of "*the pastures of God*," alluding to the Promised Land of Israel.

Asaph, the Psalmist states that this coalition takes "crafty counsel against Your people," alluding to the Jews. The Hebrew words can also be translated as they, *conspire together in secret and make shrewd plans.*

This confederacy fails to realize that you can't keep a secret from God, especially when it comes to crafting shrewd plans for wiping Israel off of the map.

> "But I, the Lord, search all hearts and examine secret
> motives. I give all people their due rewards, according to
> what their actions deserve."
> (Jeremiah 17:10, NLT)

Thus, through Psalm 83 God reveals the coming clandestine plans of these conspiring belligerents. Later on in this chapter, we will discover what *"due rewards"* their evil *"actions deserve."*

Before unveiling the members of this confederacy let's make some obvious observations.

1. In order to wipe Israel off of the map, the nation of Israel must first exist on the map.
2. Between 135 A.D to 1948 A.D. most world maps displayed the name of Palestine, or some lingual derivative of this name, instead of Israel. Thus, this war prophecy could not have been fulfilled during this past 1813-year timespan.

3. However, in May of 1948 the nation of Israel reappeared on international maps. Thus, with the weaponries of today a plot to "*cut them off from being a nation, that the name of Israel may be remembered no more,*" although unrealistic, is viable.

4. In order to secretly plot against the Jews in order to "*cut them off from being a nation,*" there must be Jews living in Israel that can be cut off, or in other words, killed. Adolph Hitler was unsuccessful in his bid to commit Jewish genocide, and as a result of his failure, Jews living in the nation of Israel is a reality today, which means this prophecy can now happen.

The Confederacy of Psalm 83

Who are these confederates who dare to think that they could wipe Israel off of the world maps and historical pages of time? They are identified by their ancient names below.

> "The tents of Edom and the Ishmaelites; Moab, and the Hagarenes; Gebal, and Ammon, and Amalek; Philistia with the inhabitants of Tyre: Assyria also is joined with them; They have helped the children of Lot. *Selah*"
> (Psalm 83:6-8, ASV)

When the Psalmist issued this prophecy, these historic names were all he knew. Thus we need to identify their modern-day equivalents. This ten-member confederacy likely consists of the following countries and the terrorist groups inhabiting them. In the image, they are listed in their ordering within the passage above because understanding their placements within the grouping typically tells the tale of whose leading the charge.

The Psalm 83 Confederates

The Psalm 83 Confederates

Tents of Edom	Palestinians & Southern Jordanians
Ishmaelites	Saudis (Ishmael father of the Arabs)
Moab	Palestinians & Central Jordanians
Hagarenes	Egyptians (Hagar Egyptian Matriarch)
Gebal	Northern Lebanese, maybe Hezbollah
Ammon	Palestinians & Northern Jordanians
Amalek	Arabs of the Sinai & Negev Desert
Philistia	Gaza, might include Hamas
Tyre	Southern Lebanese, maybe Hezbollah
Assyria	Syrians & Iraqis

The Tents of Edom and the Palestinian Refugees Connection

At the top of the list are, "The tents of Edom." On ancient Middle East maps, Edom was located in what is now Southern Jordan. Through several waves of migration in past history, many Edomites moved into Israel. Presently, the Edomites have an ethnical remnant within the Palestinians.

In my *Psalm 83: The Missing Prophecy Revealed* book in the chapter entitled, "The Whodomites, Who are the Edomites Today," I trace the trail from the ancient Edomites into today's Palestinian refugees. I believe if Asaph were alive today, he would identify "The tents of Edom" as the Palestinian refugees.

It's important to note that the Edomites are listed first within the coalition. Whenever a population or a nation is identified first in the Bible, it makes them the star of the show, or in this case the leading actor in the Middle East theater. It's similar to the credits at the end of a movie, which starts with the leading actors and is followed by the supporting cast.

Also, the Edomites are identified as tent-dwellers, which is a biblical typology for refugees. Thus, it appears that the plight of the Palestinian refugees could be the driving force behind the formation of the confederacy and its plans to destroy the Jewish state. Thus, the apparent goal is to get rid of Israel and replace it with another Mideast Arab state called Palestine.

(The image is of the Jaramana Palestinian refugee camp that was established in 1948)[27]

The Palestinians living in tents became a reality after the Arabs were defeated in their war against Israel in 1948.

The map below, which superimposes the ancient names upon their modern-day equivalents, illustrates that the Psalm 83 confederacy forms an inner circle of countries that mostly share common borders with Israel. This is important to note because none of these are in the outer ring of nations in the Ezekiel 38 prophecy, which is the subject covered in a later chapter within this book. The Ezekiel 38 map is also displayed below for comparison.

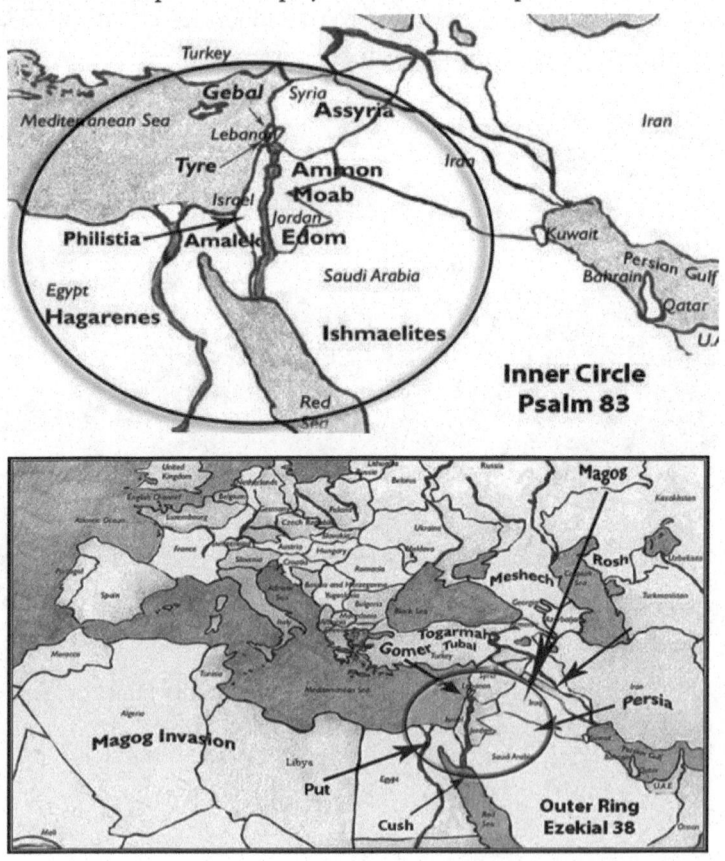

Inner Circle Psalm 83

Outer Ring Ezekial 38

(The above "Outer Ring" map of the Ezekiel 38 coalition superimposes the ancient names upon their modern-day equivalents).

The Inhabitants of Tyre and Hezbollah Terrorist Organization Connection

Within the Psalm 83 confederacy another group is listed as dwelling in a habitation condition. Edom was identified by tent-dwellers, but Tyre is distinguished by its "inhabitants." The Hebrew word for inhabitants is *"yashab"*[28] and it shows up hundreds of times in the Old Testament. The term can be used to identify a group that has been resettled as occupants and subsequently become elevated into a position of authority.

As the inner circle Psalm 83 map displays, Tyre is in Lebanon, which is the country that the Hezbollah Terrorist Organization inhabits. Hezbollah is a militant Islamic group that was established by Iran. Hezbollah was behind the 1983 US embassy attack in Beirut.

Hezbollah has developed a powerful military that includes an estimated 150,000 advanced missiles, some of which are precision-guided.

"Israel raises Hezbollah rocket estimate to 150,000" (Times of Israel – 11/12/15)

"Hezbollah chief boasts of drones, precision-guided missiles" (AP – 2/16/22)

In addition to having a strong military presence, Hezbollah has also developed a powerful political and social position within Lebanon, which has earned them the reputation of being "a state within a state." If Psalm 83 happens and Hezbollah still exists at the time, then this terrorist organization is likely the group Asaph was identifying for us as the inhabitants of Tyre.

Before moving into the next subject, it's important to note that if the "tents of Edom" represent the Palestinian refugees and if the "inhabitants of Tyre" are the Hezbollah, then both groups exist today. Moreover, the Palestinians desperately want a state of their own within Israel and with Jerusalem as their capital city. If Israel gets eliminated, that's even more in line with their wishes. In fact, the Palestinian school textbooks don't even include Israel in the Middle East maps.

> *"One day, a young Palestinian will raise the Palestinian flag over Jerusalem, the eternal capital of the state of Palestine!" (Mahmood Abbas 2012)*

> *"Israel Not On Map in Palestinian Textbooks" (Washington Post – 9/3/2000)*

Furthermore, Hezbollah continually banners the Palestinian plight in its quest for statehood.

> *"Nasrallah Lauds Palestinians' Heroism, Reiterates Hezbollah's Support for Palestine" (Tasnim News Agency – 4/12/22)*

Thus far in this chapter the identities, not the specific futures, of the Psalm 83 confederates have been revealed. The "tents of Edom" and the "inhabitants of Tyre" were specifically singled out because Asaph felt it was important to list them in a habitation condition. However, these are only two of the ten-membered Arab confederacy.

The prior chapter entitled, "The War Between Israel and Syria," explained what the future holds for Syria, a third member of the confederacy. In the upcoming chapters that connect the related peripheral prophecies to Psalm 83, I will unpack the war prophecies that deal with the other seven members: Jordan, Egypt, Syria, Saudi Arabia, the Hamas in Gaza and the Palestinians.

The War of Psalm 83

Obviously, the Arab confederacy's goal to wipe Israel off the map can't be accomplished through a politically brokered "Two State Solution," which is what the international community favors. Many world leaders, including several modern-day American presidents leading the charge, fantasize that the Jews and Palestinians can live side by side in peace within their own two separate states.

After decades of failed diplomacy, the political push for a "Two State Solution" has only intensified the problems in the Mideast. It has led the Palestinians and their Arab supporters, which includes the members of the Psalm 83 confederacy, to propagate the myth that the Palestinians have rightful claims of ownership over lands in Israel. Meanwhile, Israel is preparing for a war with Iran, its proxies and anybody else that wants to wipe the Jewish state off of the map.

Diplomacy is not the only way to resolve a matter and when it fails, wars begin and war is what Psalm 83:9-18 predicts will happen. The Arab-Israeli conflict will only end when the Israeli Defense Forces defeat their Arab foes. The specific details of these battles are found in several related peripheral prophecies. In the end analysis there will be no Palestine and instead of Israel being blotted off the map, the Jewish state will expand its borders incrementally into some parts of the Promised Land. These IDF victories and territorial expansions are the subjects of the next few chapters.

Now that we have identified the *Arab confederacy* and their *plot*, it's time to discover the details and end results of this final conflict. The remainder of this chapter is broken into the following two sections:

- The War Details: Psalm 83:9-12 – the petition to empower the IDF to victory,
- The End Results: Psalm 83:13-18 – the recognition that the LORD is GOD.

The War Details: Psalm 83:9-12 – the Petition to Empower the IDF to Victory

"Deal with them as *with* Midian, As *with* Sisera, As *with* Jabin at the Brook Kishon, Who perished at En Dor, *Who* became *as* refuse on the earth. Make their nobles

> like Oreb and like Zeeb, Yes, all their princes like Zebah and Zalmunna, Who said, "Let us take for ourselves The pastures of God for a possession.""
> (Psalm 83:9-12)

Psalm 83:9-12 draws our attention to the historical battles in the book of Judges chapters 4–8. Asaph states that these past oppressors of Israel "*became as refuse on the earth.*" Some Bible translations interpret this as "*dung upon the earth.*" This disastrous condition describes the death and decay of the slain corpses of the warring troops that came against Israel. This acknowledgment sets the tone for how the Arab confederacy of Psalm 83 will be punished! They will likewise become "*as refuse on the earth!*"

But how did these ancient Arab oppressors of Israel meet their end? The answers are found in the summary of accounts below, which point out that the LORD empowered the IDF at that time to win decisive victories.

Gideon vs the Midianites - Judges, chapters 6-8, informs us that the Midianites had oppressed the Israelites for seven years. Outmanned and outgunned by 400 to 1, Gideon took three hundred warriors and destroyed 120,000 Midianites.[29] Through Gideon, the LORD reduced the Midianites *to refuse on the earth,* so that they were incapable of further aggression against the Jews. As a result, the Midianites never oppressed the Israelites again. (The Midianite war was detailed in the earlier chapter of this book entitled, The Past War Prophecies).

The same holds true in the Israelite-Canaanite war described in Judges 4-5. The Canaanites oppressed the Israelites for twenty years. Subsequently, the Canaanites suffered a bitter defeat by Barak and the "IDF" of that time. Like the Midianites, the Canaanites became *refuse on the earth,* and never oppressed the Jewish people again.

In both examples, the Israelites were operating under divine empowerment and protection. Additionally, both enemies of Israel were defeated from top to bottom. Even their kings, nobles, and princes were killed alongside their soldiers. Importantly, these particular enemies ceased to ever oppress the Israelites or their Promised Land again.

Since the Psalm 83 confederates, including their leaders, (*kings, nobles, and princes*), have not yet been reduced to *refuse upon the earth*, we can conclude that Asaph's pleadings in Psalm 83:9-12 are still unanswered and as such, the entirety of the Psalm 83 prophecy remains unfulfilled. This means that those who believe Psalm 83 has been completely fulfilled in the past Arab-Israeli wars of 1948, 1967 and 1973 are apparently mistaken. Moreover, Psalm 83:13-18 also argues strongly against the possibility that Psalm 83 has found final fulfillment.

The End Results: Psalm 83:13-18 – the Recognition that the LORD is GOD

> "O my God, make them (*the Arab confederacy*) like the whirling dust, Like the chaff before the wind! As the fire burns the woods, And as the flame sets the mountains on fire, So pursue them with Your tempest, And frighten them with Your storm."
> (Psalm 83:13-15; emphasis added)

In the process of the mighty Psalm 83 Arab confederacy being reduced to *refuse on the earth*, the passage above uses war imageries that help portray the conditions of the conflict.

- "*The whirling dust, Like the chaff before the wind,*" pictures the Arab armies being blown away and forced to scatter, which will lead to their surrender.
- "*As the fire burns the woods, And as the flame sets the mountains on fire,*" alludes to a massive war fought with weapons capable of destroying many troops and burning up sizable portions of enemy territory.

- *"So pursue them with Your tempest, And frighten them with Your storm,"* depicts the enemy armies fleeing in fear for their lives.

A couple of parallel passages with the same imageries of fire and flames, which find a specific application to this battle are below.

"The house of Jacob, (*the IDF*), shall be *a fire*, And the house of Joseph, (*the IDF*)*, a flame*; But the house of Esau, (*the Palestinians*), *shall be* stubble; They shall kindle them and devour them, And no survivor shall *remain* of the house of Esau," For the Lord has spoken."
(Obadiah 1:18, emphasis added)

"In that day I will make the governors of Judah, (*the IDF*), like *a firepan* in the woodpile, and like *a fiery* torch in the sheaves; they shall devour all the surrounding peoples, (*The Psalm 83 Arab confederates*), on the right hand and on the left, (*the inner circle of Arabs*), but Jerusalem shall be inhabited again in her own place—Jerusalem."
(Zechariah 12:6; emphasis added)

The forthcoming chapters that deal with the peripheral prophecies of Psalm 83 will include many more parallel passages like these two above.

"Fill their, (*The Psalm 83 Arab confederates*), faces with shame, That they may seek Your name, (*Jehovah and not Allah*), O Lord. Let them be confounded and dismayed forever; Yes, let them be put to shame and perish, That they may know that You, whose name alone *is* the Lord, *Are* the Most High, (*one true God*), over all the earth."
(Psalm 83:16-18; emphasis added)

In these three concluding verses of Psalm 83, Asaph petitions the LORD to *"put to shame"* and cause the Arab confederates to *"perish,"* which means to become *refuse on the earth*. Asaph wants the Arab survivors to become confounded by the overwhelming defeat of their armies. He wants these defeated Arabs to be so deeply dismayed and disturbed that they finally realize their Allah is not most high over all the earth, but is only a false god.

Once they understand the lie about Allah, Asaph hopes that these Arab remnants "*may know that You, (Jehovah) whose name alone is the Lord, Are the Most High over all the earth.*"

The Bible acknowledges that there will be Arab remnants that abandon Allah and worship the LORD, but as we just studied, they will learn the hard way. They will witness their armies become *refuse on the earth* and the Israeli Defense Forces emerge into an exceedingly great army, in fulfillment of Ezekiel 37:10.

The verses below summarize what happens when Psalm 83 finally happens.

> "This they shall have for their pride, Because they have reproached and made arrogant threats Against the people of the Lord of hosts. The Lord *will be* awesome to them, For He will reduce to nothing all the gods of the earth; *People* shall worship Him, Each one from his place, Indeed all the shores of the nations."
> (Zephaniah 2:10-11)

In "*their pride*" the Arab confederacy "*reproached and made arrogant threats*" against the Jews. They plotted to wipe Israel off the map and they erroneously thought their god Allah would intervene and lead them to victory in Psalm 83. But no, instead the LORD Jehovah, "*the Most High over all the earth,*" empowers the IDF to a decisive victory over these Arab armies. As a result they watch Allah lose his Akbar, (his greatness), as he gets reduced to nothing!

God's Role in Psalm 83

The LORD will get drawn into this war in order to protect the nation of Israel from being wiped off the map and to prevent the annihilation of the Jewish people. This is why Asaph petitions God emphatically in Psalm 83:1. *"Do not keep silent, O God! Do not hold Your peace, And do not be still, O God!"* If the LORD does not intervene in this final war, then Israel would be at high risk of being eliminated.

Presently, that's exactly what Rabbi Shmuel Rabinovitch is worried about. That's why on May 3, 2022, at the annual Western Wall memorial service for Israel's fallen soldiers, he read Psalm 83 in front of rows of Israeli political leaders and IDF captains and soldiers. This was a significant reading because he is the Rabbi of the Western Wall and Holy Sites in Israel. He escorts visiting heads of state and foreign dignitaries during visits to the Wall.[30]

In an article entitled, *"Psalm 83 and Israel's Memorial Day,"* Israel Today, a news agency based in Jerusalem, posted this news story about the significance of this specific reading. Below is a quote from this article that was written by Ryan Jones.

> *"Modern reality continues to echo the Bible, as enemies long to "destroy them as a nation, so that Israel's name is remembered no more." So even after 25 years in Israel, it still struck me anew on Tuesday evening to hear Rabbi Shmuel Rabinovitch, rabbi of the Western Wall, fully recite Psalm 83 during the official state ceremony marking the start of Israel's Memorial Day, as lines of IDF soldiers stood at attention next to him. And it wasn't just a frivolous reading of scripture. The rabbi used the psalmist's words to plead afresh with the Almighty to come to Israel's aid... For just as the in days when Psalm 83 was penned,... Now we face the likes of the Ayatollahs, Hamas, and Hezbollah."*

It's important to note that only a few days after Rabbi Rabinovitch's quote, the Israeli Defense Forces started its largest military drill ever in its history called, "Chariots of Fire." The drill was aimed at targeting Iran's nuclear program and it also geared up for a retaliatory war with Iran's proxies of Hezbollah, Syria, Hamas etc. Read the related headlines below.

> *"IDF opens largest training drill in Israeli history"… "Chariots of Fire" (Jerusalem Post – 5/9/22)[31]*
>
> *"Israel to Simulate Massive Military Strike on Iran as Nuclear Fears Grow" (Newsweek – 5/17/22)[32]*
>
> *"IDF drills for multi-front war, including 1,500 rockets a day fired from Lebanon"*
>
> *"During monthlong exercise simulating war against Hezbollah on northern frontier, military prepares for heavy damage, hundreds of casualties, and finds issues with logistics." (Times of Israel – 5/27/22)[33]*

It's likely that Rabbi Rabinovitch was aware of this military exercise when he decided to recite Psalm 83 before the very IDF captains and soldiers that would be involved in this massive preparatory war effort. The Rabbi's timely reading in conjunction with Israel's largest military drill suggests that the Psalm 83 war still remains unfulfilled.

In reality, the Psalm 83 war doesn't have to happen because the LORD prepared a pathway to peace in the Middle East and it is foretold over 2600 years ago in Jeremiah 12:14-17. He has already set the miraculous wheels in motion, but when you understand the terms of this plan you discover that the Arabs are not, and will not, comply to their obligations.

If you want to learn more about the LORD's compassionate Mideast peace plan, it's detailed in Jeremiah 12:14-17 and explained in the next chapter entitled, "*God's Middle East Peace Plan.*"

The Psalm 83 Objections

There are commentators that don't believe Psalm 83 is a prophecy, but is only an imprecatory prayer, in which Asaph petitions the LORD to intervene on behalf of Israel to eliminate their general enemies. Then, there are some who think it's already happened in ancient and / or modern history. A few others consider it to be a prophecy that finds fulfillment as part of the Ezekiel 38 prophecy.

I have considered their arguments and believe that they are incorrect. I do agree that Psalm 83 is a prayer, but I believe that it is also a prophecy. As such, I have included an appendix in this book entitled, *"Why Psalm 83 is a Prayer and a Future War Prophecy."* Additionally, I have produced a video entitled, *"Why Psalm 83 is an unfulfilled and stand-alone prophecy,"* which also addresses the arguments above. You can view this video at this weblink: https://www.youtube.com/watch?v=iN_dKFhNOyU&t=8s.

Did the War of 1948 Fulfill Psalm 83?

One objection to the interpretation that Psalm 83 is a future war prophecy is that it was completely fulfilled in the Arab-Israeli wars of 1948. If it was fulfilled in the past, as some suggest then, how was it so vastly overlooked by the prophecy teachers in the 40's, 50's, 60's, 70's, 80's, 90's, etc.

In contrast, most of the prophecy experts who now say Psalm 83 was fulfilled in this past war are among those who, during those decades, trumpeted the rebirth of Israel in 1948 as the super-sign of the end times. Why didn't these prophecy teachers also trumpet their opinions that the fulfillment of Psalm 83 was also a tandem super-sign of the end times?

It wasn't until after 2008 that these teachers began saying that the Psalm 83 prophecy was fulfilled in Israel's past wars, which was the year that I published my book entitled, *Isralestine, the Ancient Blueprints of the Middle East.* Psalm 83 was the central theme within *Isralestine.*

One popular Bible prophecy teacher that believes Psalm 83 was fulfilled in 1948 is Amir Tsarfati. In his April 14, 2023, article entitled, *"Why I Believe We are Not Watching the Fulfillment of Psalm 83,"* he states the following.

> "*Many have contacted me recently asking if Israel's current perilous situation could bring about the fulfillment of Psalm 83. I tell them no. Why? Primarily because Psalm 83 was already fulfilled 75 years ago...Despite the best efforts of Israel's enemies, they were no match for an all-powerful God who was fulfilling His promises to the tiny nation. As in Psalm 83, the people called out for divine assistance, and it was given.*"

The good news about Amir is that at least he agrees with me that the Psalm is a prophecy, but where we split on this issue is that I don't believe Psalm 83 found final fulfillment in 1948.

Why the 1948 Arab-Israeli War did not fulfill Psalm 83

In the war of 1948 the motive of Psalm 83, which is to wipe Israel off of the map, was present and the confederacy of Psalm 83:5-8 was aligned, which is why some believe that war fulfilled the prophecy. However, the results that are petitioned for in Psalm 83:9-18 were never accomplished.

When this war prophecy finds fulfillment then these Arab countries will be so soundly defeated that they will never be able to oppress Israel again. Like the Canaanites were defeated in Judges 4-5 and the Midianites in Judges 6-8, these Arabs will likewise be conquered. Both the Canaanites and Midianites were so heavily defeated that they never again could oppress Israel. This is exactly what Asaph petitions for in Psalm 83:9-18.

Important things that mitigate against the 1948 war fulfilling the entirety of Psalm 83 are below.

1. The lead member identified as the "*tents of Edom*" in Psalm 83:6 seems to identify the Palestinian refugees as tent dwellers. As a result of the 1948 war, these refugees became a tent-dwelling reality. Thus, the *tents of Edom* didn't seem to exist during the war of 1948, but only after that

war. Now that these Palestinian refugees exist, they can participate in their role as the *tents of Edom* when Psalm 83 finds its future fulfillment.

2. The 1967 and 1973 wars followed and they evidenced that some of the Psalm 83 confederate members, namely Syria, Egypt and Jordan were still able to oppress Israel. Thus, the Psalm 83:9-18 verses, which address the end of the oppression were not fulfilled.

Why Psalm 83 and Ezekiel 38 are NOT the Same War Prophecy

In an upcoming chapter you will read about the Ezekiel 38 war prophecy. Some teach that this war is the same as Psalm 83. However there are stark differences between these two wars. These dissimilarities are identified below.

1. DIFFERENT ENEMIES: Psalm 83 is a war between confederating Arab countries that share common borders with Israel. They form an inner circle of nations and these have been Israel's notorious enemies since time immemorial. In contrast, the Ezekiel 38 coalition consists of mostly non-Arab nations that share no borders with Israel. They form an outer ring of nations who have not been historical enemies of Israel.

2. DIFFERENT MOTIVES: The goal of the Psalm 83 countries is to wipe Israel off of the map and to take the land of Israel for their possession as per Psalm 83:4, 12. Contrarily, the motive for the Ezekiel 38 invaders is to conquer Israel for plunder and booty as per Ezekiel 38:12-13.

3. DIFFERENT DEFEATS: In Psalm 83 the Israeli Defense Forces defeat the inner circle confederacy as per Zechariah 12:6, Jer. 49:2, Ezek. 25:14, Ps. 83:9-11 and elsewhere. However, in Ezekiel 38, the LORD defeats the invaders

supernaturally, through a great earthquake, flooding rains, great hailstones, fire and brimstone as per Ezek. 38:19-22.

4. DIFFERENT RESULTS: At the conclusion of Psalm 83 the inner circle of Arab countries will end their ancient hatred of the Jews and these Arabs will never oppress Israel again. Whereas in Ezekiel 38-39 the LORD will make His Holy Name Known.

> "So I will make My holy name known in the midst of My people Israel, and I will not let them profane My holy name anymore. Then the nations shall know that I am the Lord, the Holy One in Israel."
> (Ezekiel 39:7)

10

God's Middle East Peace Plan

(Jeremiah 12:14-17)

It was mid-April of 2014 and I was on the set of the Daystar show entitled, "Marcus and Joni." They were interviewing me about the impending Mideast-related Bible prophecies to be on the lookout for. One of the questions Joni asked me was, "If I could speak directly to (the then presiding) US Secretary of State, John Kerry, what would I tell him about how to achieve a lasting Middle East peace."

This was an especially timely question because John Kerry had reached the nine-month deadline of peace talks that began on July 29, 2013, between Israeli Prime Minister Benjamin Netanyahu and Palestinian Authority President Mahmoud Abbas. The talks were on the verge of collapsing any day at that time.

My reply to Joni's question is encapsulated and expounded upon within this chapter. I essentially told her that *"I would introduce John Kerry to God's Middle East Peace Plan provided in Jeremiah 12:14-17."*

The Kerry Peace Plan collapsed shortly after my interview. The problem with President Obama's and John Kerry's plan was that it mostly mirrored the similar failed land-for-peace policies that were attempted during the Bill Clinton and George W. Bush presidential administrations. Trading God's Promised Land for an elusive Arab peace is not the solution. It's not biblically endorsed. This chapter will present the biblically approved plan.

Part One of the Peace Plan

> "Thus says the LORD: "Against all My evil neighbors who touch the inheritance which I have caused My people Israel to inherit—behold, I will pluck them [the Arabs] out of their [the Jews] land [Israel] and pluck out the house of Judah from among them [the surrounding Arab nations]. Then it shall be, after I have plucked them out, that I will return and have compassion on them and bring them back, everyone to his heritage and everyone [Jew and Arab] to his [respective] land."
> (Jeremiah 12:14-15, NKJV; emphasis added)

The Parties to the Plan

Part one of God's plan identifies the parties. The Jews are called "My people" and the Arabs represent the "evil neighbors." This plan rises above political correctness and deals directly with the heart of the matter. The LORD realized that when He restored His people back into their Promised Land of Israel, there would be a two-fold problem.

1. First, there would be some reluctance from Jews, who had become well-established in the neighboring Arab lands during their centuries of diaspora, to abandon their homes, businesses and communities.
2. Second, there would be harsh resistance from the evil Arab neighbors who unrightfully homesteaded the Holy Land, while the Jews were dwelling outside of this land during the diaspora.

This assessment was 100% correct! In 1947, the evil neighbors all voted against UN Resolution 181, which legislated the reestablishment of the nation of Israel. Then they warred against Israel in 1948, 1967 and 1973. So let's give God credit for recognizing centuries in advance, the regional realities that would exist in 1948.

The Preparations for the Plan

During the Jewish diaspora, the Arabs essentially homesteaded the Holy Land of Israel. So, in order for God's plan to be implemented He would first need to, "pluck" the evil neighbors out of Israel to make room for the returning Jews. In addition, many Jews would need to be plucked out of the neighboring Arab territories so that the Arabs could go back to the lands of their inheritance.

This plan represents the compassionate peaceful political and spiritual solutions to the regional problems of the return of the Jew into the Holy Land. Jeremiah suggests that his God would cause the corridors to open for the Arabs to leave the land destined to become the Jewish state and return to the lands of their ancestry.

In addition, He would resettle the Jews out of the surrounding Arab nations, and bring them back into their homeland Israel. As each ethnic group migrated, they would vacate homes and jobs enabling economic opportunities for the returning peoples and in some cases, already existing communities to inhabit. These Jeremiah passages represent the ancient blueprints, divinely designed to ensure the successful return of the Jewish people back to the land of their heritage.

Observe the keyword Jeremiah uses is "pluck," which implies that the relocations of the Arabs and Jews back to their rightful places would require sovereign action by the LORD. He will need to uproot them and then transplant them. In order to implement part one of this plan the LORD had to free up all of these pertinent homelands because between 1517-1918 AD these territories were under the control of the Ottoman Empire, also known as the Turkish Empire.

Thus, first the LORD had to oust the Turks and second, He had to reestablish the Arab and Jewish states. This plan was put into sovereign place after World War I when the following countries regained their statehoods:

- Egypt – 1922,
- Saudi Arabia and Iraq – 1932,
- Lebanon – 1943,
- Syria and Jordan – 1946,
- Israel – 1948.

Jeremiah 12:15 says, "*I will return and have compassion on them and bring them back, everyone to his heritage and everyone* [Jew and Arab] *to his* [respective] *land.*" How's that for a land-for-peace solution? The remapping of the atlases after World War I makes the political land-for-peace deals of our time pale in comparison.

Part Two of the Peace Plan

> "And it shall be, if they [the resettled Arabs] will learn carefully the ways of My people, to swear by My name, 'As the LORD lives,' as they taught My people to swear by Baal, then they shall be established in the midst of My people. But if they do not obey, I will utterly pluck up and destroy that nation," says the LORD.'"
> (Jeremiah 12:16-17, NKJV; emphasis added)

Part two of God's plan provides the condition for the evil neighbors. If they want to be "established" in the Middle East as friendly neighbor nations to Israel, they need to worship Jehovah, the one true God of the Bible. They need "*to swear by My name, 'As the LORD lives.*"

Being established in this context means more than simply achieving Arab statehood, but involves receiving God's promise of "compassion" that is offered to them in Jer. 12:15. Some Bible translations interpret the phrase, "they shall be established in the midst of My people" as:

- "they will be given a place among my people." (NLT)

- "they will be built up among My people." (HCSB)
- "they will be built up in the midst of My people." (NASB)

This requested worship of Jehovah needs to be sincere and presented with the full zeal that the Jews of Jeremiah's time offered up to the false Arab god named Baal. At that former time, the apostate Jews were so devoted to Baal that they were sacrificing their children to him.

> "They have also built the high places of Baal, to burn their sons with fire *for* burnt offerings to Baal, which I did not command or speak, nor did it come into My mind."
> (Jer. 19:5)

Jeremiah is not suggesting the evil neighbors perform child sacrifices to Jehovah, but he is instructing them to swear by Jehovah with that comparable level of passion. This is not the case among the evil Arab neighbors today.

Thus, although the Arab states exist on the map, they are not "*established*" in the manner prescribed in Jer. 12:15-16. They are not recipients of the national blessings from God's "*compassion*." The Arabs have been brought "*back, everyone to his heritage and everyone to his land*," but they are not swearing their allegiance to Jehovah, the God of the Bible, rather they are full-heartedly worshipping Allah, the false god of the Koran.

Further hindering being "*established*" as a neighborly nation by God to His standards, is the fact that the Arab states, by and large, are refusing to receive the Palestinian refugees into their countries. These Palestinians are also incorporated into the clause of God's peace plan that says, "*everyone to his heritage and everyone to his land.*"

God's peace plan does not include any provisions for these Arab refugees. They likewise, need to be absorbed back into the lands of their heritage, which in large part includes modern-day Jordan.

Thus, it's a double whammy of non-compliance by the evil neighbors. They don't *"swear by My name, 'As the Lord lives,"* and they are blocking out a large segment of Arabs from returning to the lands of their heritage. Making these evil neighbors more wicked is that they support and promote the misguided mindset of the displaced Palestinian refugees, which is that the land of their heritage is the nation of Israel.

Foreknowing the evil neighbors would not act in accordance with God's Mideast Peace Plan, it concludes with a precautionary provision, which stipulates, *"But if they do not obey, I will utterly pluck up and destroy that* [evil neighbor] *nation," says the Lord."*

Conclusion

The Middle East conflict that confounds the politicians today has not caught God off guard. The biblical peace plan took into consideration that there would be "evil neighbors" residing within the holy land. He foreknew they would need to be relocated to make way for the return of the Jewish people.

Provisions were included in Jeremiah's prophecy for their future as well. They would be **"plucked out"** and resettled in their former homelands. A fertile future awaited them, if they entreated their affections to Jehovah, Jeremiah's God. These evil neighbors were offered the following benefits in God's Mideast Peace Plan, they:

1. Get to return to the *lands* of their *heritage* after residing centuries without a homeland,
2. Would witness and be able to receive God's *compassion* throughout the process,
3. Could mend their former ways and swear allegiance to Jehovah, the one true God,
4. Can become *established* as blessed neighborly nations alongside Israel.

In retrospect, we now realize that rather than capitalizing on these peace plan benefits, they continue to act out as "evil neighbors." In this condition, they are:

1. Currently being deprived of God's wonderful "compassions,"
2. Not qualified to be "established" as a good neighborly nation to Israel,
3. Will utterly be plucked up and destroyed.

The destructions of these evil neighbors are the subject of the next two chapters.

11

Israel Defeats the Surrounding Arab Armies

(Zechariah 12:1-6)

The prior chapter points out that Jeremiah 12:17 declared, *"But if they* (the evil Arab neighbors) *do not obey, I will utterly pluck up and destroy that nation," says the Lord."* This chapter will put forward the prophecies related to the destructions of the evil Arab neighbor nations. I identify these foretellings as the Psalm 83 peripheral prophecies because these nations, and terrorist organizations within them are all members of the Psalm 83:5-8 Arab confederacy.

These evil neighbor nations are the subject of the Ezekiel prophecy below.

> ""And there shall no longer be a pricking brier or a painful thorn for the house of Israel from among all *(those evil neighbors) who are* around them, who despise them. Then they shall know that I *am* the Lord God."
> 'Thus says the Lord God: "When I have gathered the house of Israel from the peoples among whom they are scattered, and am hallowed in them in the sight of the Gentiles, then they will dwell in their own land which I gave to My servant Jacob. And they will dwell safely there, build houses, and plant vineyards; yes, they will

dwell securely, when I execute judgments on all those around them who despise them. Then they shall know that I *am* the Lord their God." ' "
(Ezekiel 28:24-26)

Ezekiel points out that the Jews will be regathered *"from the peoples among whom they are scattered."* They will come out of their diaspora and *"dwell in their own land."* Then these regathered Jews will *"build houses, and plant vineyards."* These things have been primarily happening since May 14, 1948, when Israel was reestablished as the Jewish state.

Ezekiel further states that the time will come when Israel will, *"dwell safely"* and *"securely,"* which is not the case today. The reason Israel doesn't *"dwell safely"* and *"securely"* presently is because the evil neighbors, *"who are around them"* *"despise them"* and serve as *"a pricking brier or a painful thorn"* in Israel's side. That's all about to change because the Lord is going to, *"execute judgments on all those around them who despise them."*

The tool the Lord will use to *"execute judgments on all those around them who despise them,"* is primarily the Israeli Defense Forces, which the forthcoming peripheral prophecies will point out.

The Zechariah 12:1-6 Prophecy

Before singling out the judgments upon the individual evil Arab nations, it's helpful to do a Bible study on the Zechariah 12 prophecy related to the role of the IDF in defeating, or as Zechariah 12:6 describes, *"devouring,"* the surrounding peoples. This next section explains Zechariah 12:1-6.

"The burden of the word of the Lord against Israel. Thus says the Lord, who stretches out

the heavens, lays the foundation of the earth,
and forms the spirit of man within him:"
(Zechariah 12:1)

In this opening verse Zechariah quotes from the prophet Isaiah below.

"Thus says the Lord, your Redeemer, And He who formed you from the womb: "I *am* the Lord, who makes all *things,* Who stretches out the heavens all alone, Who spreads abroad the earth by Myself.""
(Isaiah 44:24)

The reason Zechariah draws attention to Isaiah's verse is to establish a point before he issues his full prophecy about the IDF destroying the evil neighbors. That point, which will soon be revealed within this chapter, is related to Zechariah's next two verses.

"Behold, I will make Jerusalem a cup of drunkenness to all the surrounding peoples, when they lay siege against Judah and Jerusalem. And it shall happen in that day that I will make Jerusalem a very heavy stone for all peoples; all who would heave it away will surely be cut in pieces, though all nations of the earth are gathered against it."
(Zec. 12:2-3)

In these two above verses, Zechariah foretells that someday the evil neighbors will attempt to "*lay siege against Judah and Jerusalem.*" As a result, these "*surrounding peoples*" will stagger as if having become intoxicated by "*a cup of drunkenness.*"

Since 1948, these *surrounding peoples* have been contesting Israel's rightful claims to Jerusalem as the capital of the Jewish state. Ultimately, *they*, alluding to all the surrounding peoples, will confederate in a final attempt to *lay siege on Jerusalem*. According to Zechariah 12:4-6, this is when the evil neighbor nations will be utterly plucked up and destroyed.

Zechariah 12:3 states that Jerusalem will be "*a very heavy stone for all peoples*," not just the surrounding peoples. He sends a warning to "*all nations of the earth* (who) *are gathered against it.*" This pertains to the modern-day meddling below of the international community over the status of Jerusalem.

1. UN Resolution 181 of 1947 declared, "Jerusalem as a *corpus separatum* (Latin: "separate entity") to be governed by a special international regime."[34]
2. 1949 Armistice border of 1949 established a demarcation line that divided Jerusalem into an East Jerusalem and a West Jerusalem. This was the first time in history that Jerusalem had ever been divided.

Dividing the holy city of Jerusalem is not biblically endorsed and this division didn't last for long, because eighteen years later the IDF won the Six-Day War in June of 1967 and at that time Israel captured all of Jerusalem. Although presently, all of the "*surrounding peoples*" and most "*all nations of the earth*" don't recognize Jerusalem as the undivided capital of the Jewish state, all of these peoples are sorely mistaken.

3. The unratified Arab Peace Initiative of 2002, as well as the failed American land for peace plans formed by Presidents Bill Clinton of 2000, George W. Bush of 2002 and Barrack Obama of 2014 have all attempted to keep Jerusalem as a divided city.

It's safe to say that Jerusalem has been "*a very heavy stone for all peoples; all who would heave it away.*" But why is the holy city of Jerusalem such a burdensome stone? Now it's time to reveal why Zechariah 12:1 quoted Isaiah 44:24.

Jerusalem belongs to the Jews

The reason that Zechariah opens up his prophecy by quoting Isaiah 44:24 is to establish the prophetic precedent that Jerusalem belongs to the Jews and not their evil Arab neighbors. By drawing our attention to Isaiah 44:24, we should feel compelled to read the full prophecy in Isaiah 44:24-28. When we do we arrive at the historically and prophetically proven conclusion that the LORD has given Jerusalem exclusively to the Jews. Unraveling the prophecy explains why.

The Isaiah 44:24-28 Prophecy

> "Thus says the LORD, your Redeemer, And He who formed you from the womb: "I *am* the LORD, who makes all *things,* Who stretches out the heavens all alone, Who spreads abroad the earth by Myself;"
> (Isaiah 44:24)

In this first verse the LORD establishes His credentials as the Creator, "*Who makes all things,*" including all of the land that the city of Jerusalem sits upon.

> "Who frustrates the signs of the babblers, And drives diviners mad; Who turns wise men backward, And makes their knowledge foolishness; Who confirms the word of His servant, And performs the counsel of His messengers; Who says to Jerusalem, 'You shall be inhabited,' To the cities of Judah, 'You shall be built,' And I will raise up her waste places;"
> (Isaiah 44:25-26)

In this above passage, the LORD "*says to Jerusalem, 'You shall be inhabited,' To the cities of Judah, 'You shall be built,' And I will raise up her waste places.*" When Isaiah issued this prophecy between 740-700 BC, Jerusalem was inhabited by Jews and Judah was already built up and there were no waste places to raise up. Thus, this passage anticipated a future time when Jerusalem would be uninhabited and the territory of Judah would be laid to waste.

This was fulfilled over a century later when the Babylonians sacked Jerusalem, destroyed the first Jewish Temple and desolated the land of Judah. This historical episode is when the Jews were exiled into Babylonian captivity for seventy years and their land laid waste for the duration of that time. Isaiah's prophecy continues to declare the following.

> "Who says to the deep, 'Be dry! And I will dry up your rivers'; Who says of Cyrus, '*He is* My shepherd, And he shall perform all My pleasure, Saying to Jerusalem, "You shall be built," And to the temple, "Your foundation shall be laid." '"
> (Isaiah 44:27-28)

In this concluding prophetic passage, Isaiah predicts that Cyrus, who was the great Persian King who conquered the Babylonians in 539 BC, would be used to fulfill Isaiah's prophecy about Jerusalem being rebuilt and reinhabited by the Jews. King Cyrus wasn't even born at the time of Isaiah's prophecy, but upon discovering that Isaiah had foretold of his victory almost two hundred years in advance, he made certain to fulfill his prophetic role to have Jerusalem rebuilt and Judah reinhabited.

This historical account is recorded in the passage below.

> "…the Lord stirred up the spirit of Cyrus king of Persia, so that he made a proclamation throughout all his kingdom, and also *put it* in writing, saying, Thus says Cyrus king of Persia:"
> (Ezra 1:1-2 abbreviated)

> "All the kingdoms of the earth the Lord God of heaven has given me. And He has commanded me to build Him a house at Jerusalem which *is* in Judah. Who *is* among you of all His (*Jewish*) people? May his God be with him, and let him go up to Jerusalem which *is* in Judah, and build the house of the Lord God of Israel (He *is* God), which *is* in Jerusalem. And whoever is left in any place where he dwells, let the men of his place help him with silver and

gold, with goods and livestock, besides the freewill
offerings for the house of God which *is* in Jerusalem."
(Ezra 1:3-4, NKJV; emphasis added)

King Cyrus fulfilled the Isaiah 44:24-28 prophecy around 538 BC, which was over a decade before Zechariah 12 was even written.[35] In other words, Isaiah 44:24-28 was no longer a prophecy, but had become a matter of historical record. In fact, Zechariah was alive to witness the fulfillment of Isaiah's prophecy through King Cyrus. Zechariah was a benefactor of King Cyrus's edict to send the Jews back to reinhabit Jerusalem and rebuild Judah. Zechariah was living proof that Jerusalem and Judah was home exclusively to the Jews.

By quoting Isaiah 44:24, Zechariah, in Zec. 12:1, established absolute authority that the geopolitical status of Jerusalem and Judah was not debatable by the surrounding evil Arab neighbors nor the international community. Therefore, he proceeds to warn in Zec. 12:2-3 that Jerusalem will be a cup of trembling to the "*surrounding peoples*" and a burdensome stone to "*all peoples.*"

The IDF "shall devour all the surrounding peoples"

The surrounding Arab leaders and their armies have no idea what's going to happen to them in their final bid to lay siege against Judah and Jerusalem. The IDF, with the LORD's divine intervention, is going to win a war that will end the Arab-Israeli conflict once and for all. The apparent sequence of events that take place in this final battle are described in the passages that follow.

> ""In that day," says the Lord, (*when the surrounding peoples lay siege against Judah and Jerusalem*), "I will strike every horse with confusion, and its rider with madness; I will open My eyes on the house of Judah, and will strike every horse of the peoples with blindness.""
> (Zechariah 12:4, NKJV; emphasis added)

Divine Military Intervention

1. <u>STRIKE ONE:</u> First, it appears that the Lord causes the Arab artilleries, tanks and armored vehicles to malfunction. *"I will strike every horse with confusion,"* (Zec. 12:4a).

Remember that when Zechariah wrote, the soldiers rode into battle upon horses, rather than flew in on fighter Jets or drove military tanks. Thus, in fulfillment of Zechariah 12:2 that stated, *"Behold, I will make Jerusalem a cup of drunkenness,"* the LORD will level the field by somehow tweaking the attacking Arab's war machines.

The LORD has employed this proven tactic successfully before when Pharaoh and his Egyptian army attempted to kill Moses and the Jews at the Red Sea about three thousand years ago during the Hebrew exodus out of Egypt.

> "Now it came to pass, in the morning watch, that the Lord looked down upon the army of the Egyptians through the pillar of fire and cloud, and He troubled the army of the Egyptians. And He took off their chariot wheels, so that they drove them with difficulty; and the Egyptians said, "Let us flee from the face of Israel, the Lord fights for them against the Egyptians.""
> (Exodus 14:24-25)

Somehow, the LORD supernaturally took off the lug nuts of the Egyptian chariots and that created panic among the Egyptian troops. These Egyptian chariots were state-of-the-art at the time. Below is a quote from Wikipedia that acknowledges this.

> *"The Egyptians invented the yoke saddle for their chariot horses around 1500 BC. Chariots were effective for their high speed, mobility and strength which could not be matched by infantry at the time. They quickly became a powerful new weapon across the ancient Near East."*[36]

2. <u>STRIKE TWO:</u> Second, these armament malfunctions apparently create hysteria among the enemy soldiers like it did to the Egyptians. "*I will strike every horse with confusion and its rider with madness;*" (Zec. 12:4a,b)

The Arab armies' response to the malfunctions of their war machines in the yet future will be similar to that of the Egyptian army in the distant past. There will be panic spreading widely among the Arab troops. They will likely echo the same sentiment as the Egyptians, "*let us flee from the face of Israel, the Lord fights for them.*"

3. <u>STRIKE THREE:</u> Third, the Lord will turn His favor toward the IDF and somehow the guidance (radar) capabilities of the enemies' tanks, jets, rockets, etc. will become disabled. "*and will strike every* (enemy) *horse of the peoples with blindness.*" (Zec. 12:4d)

The Arab armies essentially STRIKE OUT before they're able to effectively go to bat---(battle) against Judah and Jerusalem. STRIKE ONE will be the war machine malfunctions. STRIKE TWO will be the madness and hysteria spread among the troops. STRIKE THREE will be the disabling of the guidance systems of their armaments.

The IDF Gains Confidence

We just read and reviewed the strike out of Zechariah 12:a,b and d, but now it's time to double back and look at Zechariah 12:c, which states; "*In that day,… I will open My eyes on the house of Judah.*" This section tells us "*in that day,*" when the Arabs make their final bid to lay siege on Judah and Jerusalem, that the LORD's eyes will be wide and his eyebrows raised to the Arab's plotting. The next Zechariah passage explains why this is important.

> "For thus says the Lord of hosts: "He sent Me after
> glory, to the nations which plunder you; *(Israel)*
> for he who touches you touches the apple of His

eye. For surely I will shake My hand against them, and they shall become spoil for their servants. Then you will know that the Lord of hosts has sent Me."
(Zechariah 2:8-9, NKJV; emphasis added)

Israel is the apple of the LORD'S eye and the Arab armies attempting to take over Judah and Jerusalem, is likened to trying to poke God's eye out. By the time all of the above in Zechariah 12:4 happens, the stage will be set for the IDF to confidently devour the surrounding peoples. The next two verses foretell how the IDF soundly defeats their evil Arab neighbors.

"And the governors of Judah shall say in their heart, 'The inhabitants of Jerusalem *are* my strength in the Lord of hosts, their God.' In that day I will make the governors of Judah like a firepan in the woodpile, and like a fiery torch in the sheaves; they shall devour all the surrounding peoples on the right hand and on the left, but Jerusalem shall be inhabited again in her own place—Jerusalem."
(Zec. 12:5-6)

The "*governors of Judah*" represent the IDF. The Hebrew word used for governors can be translated as captains or chieftains. The IDF will find "*strength in the LORD*" as they witness the LORD in action striking out the evil neighbors. A confident IDF will be like "*a firepan in the woodpile.*" They will be "*like a fiery torch in the sheaves*" as they wipe out the surrounding Arab armies "*on the right hand and on the left.*"

The Arabs will no longer be able to contest Jewish sovereignty over Jerusalem and it "*shall be inhabited again in her own place*" by Jews. In the aftermath of this IDF victory, it would not be surprising to witness the Jews demolish the Dome of the Rock, which sits atop the foundation stone of the former Jewish Temples.

Removing this Islamic religious structure would pave the way for the Jews to rebuild their Third Temple, which according to prophecies in Revelation 11:1-2, Matthew 24:15 and elsewhere will happen. The Jews are already making preparations to construct this Temple.

The next chapter will discuss the Psalm 83 peripheral prophecies related to the IDF defeats of their evil Arab neighbors "*on the right hand and on the left.*" Prior chapters covered the futures of Syria and Hezbollah in Lebanon, but now it's time to explore the war prophecies related to the Palestinians, Hamas in Gaza, Jordan, Saudi Arabia and Egypt.

12

The Psalm 83 Peripheral War Prophecies

This chapter explains the Psalm 83 peripheral war prophecies related to the Palestinians, Hamas in Gaza, Jordan, Saudi Arabia and Egypt. The peripheral prophecies are the unfulfilled foretellings involving the Psalm 83 Arab confederates that are described by various prophets. They provide additional details to the overall prophecy of Psalm 83. Some who have dismissed Psalm 83 as an unfinished prophecy, may have neglected to consider these peripheral prophecies.

Below is a relevant quote from my book entitled, *Psalm 83: The Missing Prophecy Revealed, How Israel Becomes the Next Mideast Superpower.*

"This book identifies nearly 148 verses that appear to apply to the Psalm 83 prophecy. These include prophecies from the Major Prophets including Jeremiah, Ezekiel, and Isaiah, as well as the Minor Prophets consisting of Obadiah, Zephaniah, and Zechariah. Remember that Asaph, the author of Psalm 83, is also a prophet as per 2 Chronicles 29:30. Below are just a few examples of the many passages relating to the Psalm 83 prophecy. This extensive list doesn't include the prophecies in Amos 1:1-15, which might also find application with Psalm 83.

- Psalm 83:1-18..(18 verses),
- Jeremiah 49:1-29, 12:14-17......................(33 verses),
- Ezekiel 25:12-17, 28:24-26, 35:1-36:7, 37:10 (32 verses),
- Isaiah 17:1-14, 19:1-18, 11:14...................(33 verses),

- Obadiah 1:1-21.. (21 verses),
- Zephaniah 2:4-11.......................................(8 verses),
- Zechariah 12:2,5-6..................................(3 verses).

Let's proceed to explore Psalm 83 through the details of these prophets.

The IDF vs. the Palestinians

Many of the Palestinians have descended from Esau, who fathered the Edomites. Thus, the prophecies below identify either Esau, Edom, or the Edomites. Remember, in Psalm 83:6 they are classified as "*the Tents of Edom,*" likely alluding to the Palestinian refugees of today.

> "The house of Jacob, (*the IDF*), shall be a fire, And the house of Joseph, (*the IDF*), a flame; But the house of Esau, (*the Palestinians*), *shall be* stubble; They shall kindle them and devour them, And no survivor shall *remain* of the house of Esau," For the Lord has spoken."
> (Obadiah 1:18, NKJV; emphasis added)

Above, Obadiah reveals the grim future for the Palestinian descendants of Esau. The IDF will reduce them to stubble and kindle and will devour them, which is a similar language used in Zec. 12:6. Esau will have no descendants after the IDF defeats the Palestinians.

Presently, the Palestinians seek to possess their own Arab state in the Middle East, but the next verse implies this will not likely happen.

> "Behold, I will make you, (*Edomites/Palestinians*), small among the nations; You shall be greatly despised."
> (Obadiah 1:2, NKJV; emphasis added)

Presently, the plight of the Palestinian refugees is being used by the Arab states as a buffer between them and Israel. Obadiah points this out in the verse below.

> "All the, *(Arab states)*, men in your, *(Psalm 83:5-8)*, confederacy Shall force you to the border, *(of Israel)*; The men at peace with you Shall deceive you *and* prevail against you. *Those who eat* your bread shall lay a trap for you. No one is aware of it."
> (Obadiah 1:7, NKJV; emphasis added)

Obadiah informs that the Arab states are deceiving the Palestinians and laying a trap for them. The deception, in my estimation, is the propagation of the modern-day myth that the Palestinians deserve a state within and/or adjacent to the Jewish state, which is not biblically endorsed!

Obadiah says, "*No one is aware of it.*" My translation of this statement is that; "*No one,*" especially not the Palestinians, but also neither their Arab confederacy, "*is aware*" of the dangerous folly of this deceptive behavior. Only the LORD "*is aware of it,*" and He has informed us through the peripheral prophecies of what the devastating outcome of this Palestinian trap will be.

The next passage also identifies the IDF embattling the Palestinians, and it explains that the LORD will use the IDF to execute His vengeance and fury upon them. It also informs why this judgment happens.

> "'Thus says the Lord God: "Because of what Edom did against the house of Judah by taking vengeance, and has greatly offended by avenging itself on them," therefore thus says the Lord God: "I will also stretch out My hand against Edom, cut off man and beast

from it, and make it desolate from Teman, *(Southern Jordan)*; Dedan, *(Saudi Arabia)*, shall fall by the sword. I will lay My vengeance on Edom by the hand of My people Israel, *(the IDF)*, that they may do in Edom according to My anger and according to My fury; and they shall know My vengeance," says the Lord God."
(Ezekiel 25:12-14, NKJV; emphasis added)

Southern Jordan as Edom and Teman and Saudi Arabia as Dedan, are mentioned in the above passage, which implies they are aligned with the Palestinians in the battle against Israel. Both of these countries are identified in Psalm 83. These two countries will be covered later in this chapter.

The IDF vs. Hamas in Gaza

The Hamas in Gaza are also Palestinians, so the above prophecies in Obadiah 1 and Ezekiel 25 will likely affect this terrorist organization also, that is if they are still in operation at the time these foretellings are fulfilled. Regardless, if Hamas continues to exist or someday collapses, the Palestinians in the Gaza are the subjects of the following war predictions.

Prophecies related to Gaza are identified by the ancient Philistines and the primary territories of Philistia and Gaza.

"But they, *(the IDF)*, shall fly down, *(likely in fighter jets)*, upon the shoulder of the Philistines, *(Palestinians)*, toward the west, *(in the Gaza)*; Together they shall plunder the people of the East; They shall lay their hand on Edom, *(Southern Jordan)*, and Moab, *(Central Jordan);* And the people of Ammon, *(Northern Jordan)*, shall obey them."
(Isaiah 11:14, NKJV; emphasis added)

It's important to note that Isaiah links the nation of Jordan alongside the Philistines in the Gaza. Edom, Moab, Ammon and Philistia are all part of the Psalm 83 confederacy.

> "For Gaza shall be forsaken, And Ashkelon desolate; They, *(the IDF)*, shall drive out Ashdod at noonday, And Ekron shall be uprooted. Woe to the inhabitants of the seacoast, *(Palestinians)*, The nation of the Cherethites! The word of the LORD *is* against you, O Canaan, land of the Philistines: "I will destroy you; So there shall be no inhabitant."' (Zephaniah 2:4-5, NKJV; emphasis added)

Somewhat similar to Obadiah's declaration that Esau's descendants would have no survivors, Zephaniah announces that the Palestinians living in Gaza and the neighboring cities will no longer inhabit that territory. Zephaniah 2:6-7 points out that this territory will be possessed by Israel.

The IDF vs. Jordan

Jordan is presently one of Israel's unreliable friends. On October 26, 1994, they ratified a peace treaty with Israel, but since then occasions have arisen whereby they have recalled their ambassador from Israel and members of their parliament have threatened to void out their peace agreement.

"Jordan recalls ambassador from Tel Aviv in protest over Temple Mount" (Times of Israel – 11/5/2014)

"Jordan recalls ambassador to Israel to protest detentions" (AP News – 10/29/2019)

"Jordanian parliament speaker: We oppose the peace treaty with Israel" (Jerusalem Post – 5/15/2016)

"Amid Jerusalem anger, Jordan MPs vote to review peace deal with Israel" (Times of Israel – 12/10/2017)

Ultimately, this tenuous relationship between Jordan and Israel will lead to war. Below are a couple of unfinished peripheral prophecies concerning Jordan. The foretellings clearly evidence that the peace treaty between Israel and Jordan will eventually be shattered.

The IDF vs. Northern Jordan

> "Therefore behold, the days are coming," says the Lord, "That I will cause to be heard an alarm of war In Rabbah of the Ammonites, *(Amman, Jordan)*; It shall be a desolate mound, And her villages shall be burned with fire. Then Israel shall take possession of his inheritance," says the Lord."
> (Jeremiah 49:2, NKJV; emphasis added)

Amman, the capital city of Jordan, is located in northern Jordan. It will become a *desolate mound*, much like Damascus, the capital of Syria will become as predicted in Isaiah 17:1. These two major Middle East cities are only about 141 miles apart. After desolating Amman, Israel will take possession of the city as part of the spoils of war. Jeremiah acknowledges that this city is part of Israel's inheritance because it exists within the Promised Land measured out in Genesis 15:18.

The IDF vs. Central Jordan

> "I have heard the reproach of Moab, *(Central Jordan)*, And the insults of the people of Ammon, With which they have reproached My people, *(the Jews)*, And made arrogant threats against their, *(Israel's)*, borders. Therefore, as I live," Says the Lord of hosts, the God of Israel, "Surely Moab shall be like Sodom, And the people of Ammon like Gomorrah— Overrun with weeds

and saltpits, And a perpetual desolation. The residue of My people, *(the IDF)*, shall plunder them, And the remnant of My people, *(the Jews)*, shall possess them." (Zephaniah 2:8-9, NKJV; emphasis added).

Moab and Ammon are the subjects of this prophecy. Zephaniah confirms what Jeremiah 49:2 said, which was that the Jews will win a war against Jordan and annex Ammon, but he further informs that they will also take possession of Moab. The historic territory of Moab was located in modern-day central Jordan. In other words, Israel will enlarge its borders into much of Jordan.

The Jews have a history of winning wars and capturing territory that lies within the parameters of the Promised Land. Joshua did this about 3300 years ago and King David and his son King Solomon did the same about three thousand years ago. Israel did this again after winning the Six-Day War in June of 1967. The Jews feel justified in doing this for the following reasons:

1. It increases the defensibility of their borders,
2. These are territories located within the Promised Land of Genesis 15:18 that are part of Israel's inheritance,
3. There exists historical precedence for a victorious nation to capture territory as part of the spoils of war.

Jeremiah 49:2 deals with the future of northern Jordan (Ammon). Zephaniah 2:8-9 covered both northern and central Jordan (Moab). The fate of Southern Jordan (Edom) was foretold in Ezekiel 25:14. Thus, all of Jordan will be defeated by the IDF as part of the Psalm 83 peripheral prophecies.

The IDF vs. Saudi Arabia

Saudi Arabia was the subject of Ezekiel 25:13, which was quoted earlier in this chapter. This is only one of four future prophecies related to this country. Future Saudi Arabian predictions would be under the ancient classifications of Dedan or the Ishmaelites. The first foretelling is below.

Saudi Arabia Prophecy #1

> "Flee, turn back, dwell in the depths, O inhabitants of Dedan! For I will bring the calamity of Esau upon him, The time *that* I will punish him."
> (Jer. 49:8)

This prophecy above issues a stern warning to Saudi Arabia to not get involved in the Arab confederacy of Psalm 83:5-8 and Obadiah 1:7 because the LORD says, "*I will bring the calamity of Esau upon him, The time that I will punish him.*" Therefore, the Saudis are advised to "*turn back,*" so as not to be in harm's way. The calamity and punishment of Esau, which will be against his Palestinian descendants, was previously quoted in the prophecies of Obadiah 1:18 and Ezekiel 25:13-14.

Presently, Saudi Arabia is one of the biggest supporters of the Palestinian plight. The Saudis refuse to normalize relations with Israel until the Palestinians have their own Arab state. They also put forward the Arab Peace Initiative, also known as the Saudi Initiative in 2002 for this purpose.

"Saudi FM: No normalization with Israel until Palestinian two-state solution" (i24 News – 7/24/2022)

"Saudi remains committed to Arab Peace Initiative for Israel peace, foreign minister says" (Reuters – 8/19/2020)

Saudi Arabia Prophecy #2

> "For they have consulted together with one consent; They form a confederacy against You: The tents of Edom

and the Ishmaelites; Moab and the Hagrites."
(Psalm 83:5-6)

Under the banner of the Ishmaelites, the Saudis enlist in the Arab confederacy of Psalm 83. In fact, they "are listed side by side in lockstep with the Palestinians (tents of Edom), which implies that they are inseparable. Jeremiah 49:8 warned the Saudis to *"turn back"* far from the Palestinians. He said, *"dwell in the depths,"* as a warning to leave the confederacy and send their army back home before it's too late.

Saudi Arabia Prophecy #3

"Therefore thus says the Lord God: "I will also
stretch out My hand against Edom, cut off
man and beast from it, and make it desolate
from Teman; Dedan shall fall by the sword."
(Ezekiel 25:13)

This passage was quoted earlier in this chapter in relationship to the LORD'S execution of His fury and vengeance upon Edom by the IDF. Ezekiel confirms in this verse that Dedan does not *"turn back"* and *"dwell in the depths,"* as Jeremiah warned, rather they fight in the Arab confederacy of Psalm 83. Ezekiel points out that the Saudis will *"fall by the sword,"* which means their army will be defeated.

Saudi Arabia Prophecy #4

"Sheba, *(Yemen),* Dedan, the merchants of Tarshish,
(likely the UK), and all their young lions, *(possibly the
USA),* will say to you, 'Have you, *(the Russian coalition),*
come to, *(Israel),* take plunder? Have you gathered your
army to take booty, to carry away silver and gold, to take
away livestock and goods, to take great plunder?'"
(Ezekiel 38:13, NKJV; emphasis added)

Saudi Arabia is not completely destroyed as per the Saudi Prophecy #3 because they subsequently show up in the Ezekiel 38 prophecy. The Ezekiel 38 prophecy is the subject of the next chapter. Saudi Arabia's role in Ezekiel 38:13 is that of a protestor."

One of the members alongside Dedan is called, "*the merchants of Tarshish*," which has a business-related connotation. This implies that these complaining nations have commercial interests at stake with Israel. Thus, in the fourth and final Saudi Arabia prophecy, it hints that the Saudis, after being defeated by the IDF in Psalm 83, might finally normalize relations with Israel.

The Two Future Prophecies of Egypt

Egypt is the subject of two end times judgments. The first involves a war with Israel and the second is an invasion by the Antichrist that desolates Egypt. Both of these judgment prophecies are explained exhaustively in my book entitled, *The NOW Prophecies*. Therefore, only a short explanation will be provided in this section. Like Jordan, Egypt has a fragile peace treaty with Israel that dates back to 1979, but this treaty will end according to Egypt Prophecy #1.

Egypt Prophecy #1: (IDF vs. Egypt)

> "In that day Egypt will be like women, and will be afraid and fear because of the waving of the hand of the Lord of hosts, which He waves over it. And the land of Judah, (*in Israel*), will be a terror to Egypt; everyone who makes mention of it will be afraid in himself, because of the counsel of the Lord of hosts which He has determined against it."
> (Isaiah 19:16-17, NKJV; emphasis added)

In this passage Isaiah declares that the LORD has "*determined against*" Egypt a judgment. Since this episode involves an apparent conflict with "*the land of Judah,*" which will become "*a terror to Egypt,*" These details infer that Egypt's first future judgment results from an act of Egyptian aggression against Israel.

It's likely that this aggression is manifested through Egypt's participation, under the banner of the Hagarenes, in the Psalm 83 war.

> "They have said, Come, and let us cut them off, (*the Jewish state*), from being a nation; That the name of Israel may be no more in remembrance. For they have consulted together with one consent; Against thee do they make a covenant, (*confederacy*): The tents of Edom and the Ishmaelites; Moab, and the Hagarenes."
> (Psalm 83:4-6, ASV, emphasis added)

Just like Saudi Arabia as the Ishmaelites, the Egyptians as the Hagarenes, are aligned with the Palestinian Refugees as the tents of Edom in the Arab confederacy. Hagar was the notable matriarch from Egypt, who was the mother of Ishmael. Refer to the quote below.

Barnes, Notes on the Old Testament – Ps. 83:6-8

"And the Hagarenes—The Hagarenes were properly Arabs, so called from Hagar, the handmaid of Abraham, the mother of Ishmael. Gen. 16:1; 25:12. As connected with the Ishmaelites they would naturally join in this alliance."[37]

Isaiah 19:1-15 explains the following about this future judgment upon Egypt.

1. The prophecy happens quickly, like a swift-moving cloud over the land, (Isaiah 19:1).

2. The turmoil appears to be the result of Egypt's peace accord with Israel unraveling. This causes infighting amongst brothers and neighbors, who are apparently on opposite sides of Egypt's actions against Israel. This spreads from "*city to city*" into a civil war, which then leads to a regional conflict identified as "*kingdom against kingdom*," (Isaiah 19:2).

3. In the midst of the unrest, a cruel dictator emerges, (Isaiah 19:4).

4. Then, the country experiences a severe drought that wipes out the fishing industry, (Isaiah 19:5-8).
5. This is accompanied by a total economic collapse that is so bad that, "*All who make wages will be troubled of soul,*" (Isaiah 19:9-10, 15).
6. Nobody, including their political and religious leaders, can come up with any solutions to calm the chaos, (Isaiah 19:11-13).
7. Ultimately, Egypt becomes "*as a drunken man staggers in his vomit,*" (Isaiah 19:14).

The next verse informs that the IDF wins the war and Israel captures and annexes at least five cities in the land of Egypt. The Hebrew language will be spoken within these city limits. As a memorial to Israel's victory, one of these cities will be renamed, "the City of Destruction," which implies that the IDF defeated Egypt decisively. Remember that parts of Egypt lie within the Promised Land of Genesis 15:18.

> "In that day five cities in the land of Egypt will speak the language of Canaan, (*Hebrew*), and swear by the Lord of hosts; one will be called the City of Destruction."
> (Isaiah 19:18, NKJV; emphasis added)

Concerning the great fear that overtakes Egypt in Isaiah 19:16, Dr. Arnold Fruchtenbaum says the following:

> "*Never in ancient history has this been true. Only since 1948, and especially since the 6-day war, have the Egyptian forces evidenced the fear portrayed in this passage. There has been fear and dread of Israel ever since. With Egypt having lost 4 wars against Israel with heavy casualties, the fear is deeply rooted. Prophetically, today is still the period of Isaiah 19:16-17.*"[38]

Although Egypt Prophecy #1 describes a severe judgment upon the nation, it doesn't compare to Egypt Prophecy #2.

Egypt Prophecy #2: (The Antichrist vs. Egypt)

> "He, *(the Antichrist),* shall stretch out his hand against the countries, and the land of Egypt shall not escape. He shall have power over the treasures of gold and silver, and over all the precious things of Egypt; also the Libyans and Ethiopians *shall follow* at his heels."
> (Daniel 11:42-43, NKJV; emphasis added)

Revelation 6:2 introduces the Antichrist as the "White Horseman" of the Apocalypse. It reveals that when he emerges upon the world stage that, "*he went out conquering and to conquer.*" Among his conquests is the nation of Egypt according to the passage above. As a result of his war victory over Egypt, the Egyptians become exiled and the nation becomes a wasteland. The Ezekiel passages below describe the extent of this dispersion and desolation.

> "And the land of Egypt shall become desolate and waste; then they will know that I *am* the Lord, because he said, 'The River *is* mine, and I have made *it.*' Indeed, therefore, I *am* against you and against your rivers, and I will make the land of Egypt utterly waste and desolate, from Migdol *to* Syene, as far as the border of Ethiopia. Neither foot of man shall pass through it nor foot of beast pass through it, and it shall be uninhabited forty years. I will make the land of Egypt desolate in the midst of the countries *that are* desolate; and among the cities *that are* laid waste, her cities shall be desolate forty years; and I will scatter the Egyptians among the nations and disperse them throughout the countries.'"
> (Ezekiel 29:9-12)

The prophet predicts that the country of Egypt will become a desolate wasteland for "*forty years.*" Ezekiel foretells, "*neither foot of man shall pass through it nor foot of beast pass through it, and it shall be uninhabited forty years.*" The Egyptians will be exiled "*throughout the countries*" during this entire period.

> "Yet, thus says the Lord God: "At the end of forty years I will gather the Egyptians from the peoples among whom they were scattered. I will bring back the captives of Egypt and cause them to return to the land of Pathros, to the land of their origin, and there they shall be a lowly kingdom. It shall be the lowliest of kingdoms; it shall never again exalt itself above the nations, for I will diminish them so that they will not rule over the nations anymore.""
> (Ezekiel 29:13-15)

The good news is that Egypt will be restored after the forty years have elapsed. The bad news is that Egypt will "*be the lowliest of kingdoms*" from that point forward. Presently, there is a cliché that says, "*As Egypt goes, so goes the Middle East.*" This most populous Arab country in the world has long been a bellwether for the region as a whole. However, as a result of Egypt Prophecy #2, this cliché will never be quoted again.

But when will the forty years conclude? Let's do the math.

1. The Antichrist comes on the world scene after the Rapture. Until his arrival Egypt Prophecy #2 remains unfinished.

2. Then, there appears to be a short gap of time that follows the Rapture. Some suggest it could be weeks or maybe a couple of years, and the Antichrist will be alive and well during this period.

3. The gap period ends when the Antichrist confirms the infamous false covenant between Israel and another signatory called the "many" in Daniel 9:27. This triggers the start of the Seven Year Tribulation Period.

4. Sometime within the gap period or the Tribulation Period, the Antichrist desolates Egypt and the forty years of Egyptian exile commences.

5. At the conclusion of these seven years of tribulation, the Antichrist will be cast alive into the Lake of Fire at the Second Coming of Christ as per Revelation 19:20.

6. Shortly subsequent to the Second Coming, Jesus Christ establishes His Messianic Kingdom that lasts for one thousand years as per, Rev. 20:2-7.

Therefore, unless the gap period is for a prolonged period of time, the forty years of Egypt's desolation and the correlating Egyptian dispersion ends sometime during the millennial reign of Jesus Christ. This regathering during the Millennium is somewhat supported by the next passage.

> "In that day, (*during the Millennium*), there will be a highway from Egypt to Assyria, and the Assyrian will come into Egypt and the Egyptian into Assyria, and the Egyptians will serve with the Assyrians. In that day Israel will be one of three with Egypt and Assyria—a blessing in the midst of the land, whom the Lord of hosts shall bless, saying, "Blessed is Egypt My people, and Assyria the work of My hands, and Israel My inheritance.""
> (Isaiah 19:23-25, NKJV; emphasis added)

Conclusion

This chapter has identified several unfinished prophecies that involve the participants of the Arab confederacy of Psalm 83:5-8. It has also pointed out that the IDF exists in fulfillment of Bible prophecy to conquer those Arab confederates. Therefore, unless it can be proven that any or all of the prophecies in this chapter are unrelated to Psalm 83, then the logical conclusion is that they are all Psalm 83 peripheral prophecies.

It's important to note that the Lord offered a peace plan in Jeremiah 12:14-17, but the Arab confederacy of Psalm 83 will refuse the offer. They are blinded by their perpetual hatred of Israel. So instead, they will decide to wage war against the Jewish state, and in so doing the LORD will empower the IDF, like He did in Judges chapter 4-8 and elsewhere, to decisively defeat the Arab confederacy of Psalm 83.

Ezekiel 38-39, When God Upholds His Holy Name

Up to this point, we have explored the prophecies that, when they are fulfilled, will set the stage for THE GOD of the BIBLE to make HIS HOLY NAME known to all of mankind, both Jew and Gentile. The prophecy that the LORD has chosen for this momentous occasion is foretold in Ezekiel's chapters 38 and 39.

When Ezekiel 38-39 happens, Israel will likely be responding to, and the world recovering from, the following plethora of prophetic events, (listed below in no specific chronological order);

1. Jeremiah 49:34-39, the Elam prophecy about the disaster in Iran,
2. Isaiah 17 & Jeremiah 49:23-27, the destruction of Damascus,
3. Jeremiah 49:1-6 and Zephaniah 2:8-9, the toppling of Jordan,
4. Isaiah 19:1-18, the terrorization of Egypt,
5. Psalm 83, the concluding Arab-Israeli war,
6. Obadiah 1:19-20, Jeremiah 49:2 and Zephaniah 2:9, the expansion of Israel,
7. Ezekiel 37:10, 25:14, Obadiah 1:18, the rise of the exceedingly great Israeli army,

8. 1 Corinthians 15:51-53 and 1 Thessalonians 4:15-18, the Rapture of the Church, (I, and many others, think it's possible that the Rapture could happen prior to the fulfillment of Ezekiel 38-39. If so, this is a powerful factor to add into the prophetic equation).

Ezekiel foretells that a massive coalition will form to invade Israel for plunder and booty and God will personally intervene through a powerful series of cosmic events and destroy it. This epic battle belongs to the LORD! The supernatural acts of God, which are found in Ezekiel 38:18-22, 39:2-6, will put the world on official notice that the God of the Bible is:

1. The one true God,
2. The covenant keeper of the Abrahamic covenant,
3. The promise keeper of believers in Jesus Christ.

A time is soon coming when a large and powerful group of predominately Muslim nations, none of which are listed in Psalm 83, will invade Israel. At that time, Israel will be in possession of great prosperity and these invaders will coalesce in an attempt to plunder Israel and take over great booty as their spoils of war. This confederacy, which will be led by Russia [or By Turkey], doesn't realize that the LORD is setting up a trap for them. Ezekiel 38:4 says, "*I,* (alluding to the LORD), *will turn you around, put hooks into your jaws, and lead you out, with all your army,...*" These invaders will come thinking that they can mow Israel over and run away with the spoils, but they will quickly discover, like Pharaoh and the Egyptian army did when the walls of the Red Sea collapsed and destroyed them, that the LORD is going to supernaturally slaughter them.

There exists a plethora of excellent commentaries and books written about the prophecies in Ezekiel's chapters 38 and 39, so this chapter will only provide an overview of the prophecy, but will also notate my recommended readings on the subject. I personally have written extensively about Ezekiel 38-39 in the following books:

- Psalm 83: The Missing Prophecy Revealed, How Israel Becomes the Next Mideast Superpower,
- The NOW Prophecies,
- The NEXT Prophecies.

In addition, I have authored numerous articles on the topic, which can be read from the article page on my website at www.prophecydepot.com. Moreover, for an exhaustive look at Ezekiel 38-39, I have footnoted my recommended readings on the subject.[39] Below is a nutshell outline of the Ezekiel 38-39 prophecies.

If you are unfamiliar with Ezekiel 38-39, I recommend that you read these two chapters containing fifty-two verses. In my estimation they are easy to comprehend if taken literally. You don't have to be a Bible scholar to glean what's being predicted. I think the LORD intended for these prophecies to be detail specific and understandable because this is the marquee prophecy whereby the LORD intends to accomplish the following.

> "Thus I will magnify Myself and sanctify Myself, and I will be known in the eyes of many nations. Then they shall know that I *am* the Lord."
> (Ezekiel 38:23)

> "So I will make My holy name known in the midst of My people Israel, and I will not *let them* profane My holy name anymore. Then the nations shall know that *I am* the Lord, the Holy One in Israel."
> (Ezekiel 39:7)

Ezekiel 38-39 Overview

Ezekiel 38:1-6: lists the nine-member coalition consisting of armies from Magog, Rosh, Meshech, Tubal, Persia, Ethiopia (Cush),

Libya (Put), Gomer, and Togarmah. The general consensus among the scholars is that the modern-day equivalents of these ancient populations are represented by Russia, Turkey, Iran, Libya, Ethiopia, Sudan, Somalia, Tunisia and Algeria. Some also include Germany, Morocco and some of the "stans" countries, such as Kazakhstan, Uzbekistan, Turkmenistan, Kyrgyzstan, Tajikistan and Afghanistan.

Most all commentaries connect Magog and Rosh with Russia and as such, they identify Russia as the lead nation within the coalition. This battle is often alluded to as the "Magog invasion" and the confederates are often referred to as the "Magog Invaders."

Ezekiel 38:7-10: appropriates the general conditions in Israel, the timing and the battlefield location of the invasion. The prerequisites of this prophecy are that:

1. It occurs in the latter years,
2. The nation of Israel must be reestablished,
3. The country must be located in the midst of the Promised Land,
4. The worldwide re-gathering of the Jews is underway,
5. The Israelis live in a condition of national security.

All of these five requirements must be met in order for this prophecy to find fulfillment. It is safe to assume that the first four requirements have been met. These are the latter years, Israel was restored as the Jewish State on May 14, 1948, the country is located in the center of the Promised Land and Jews have been returning steadily ever since. However, the last prerequisite does not presently exist, in my estimation. Israelis are not dwelling safely in their homeland. They live under constant threat by multiple surrounding enemies.

Specifically, Ezekiel says Israel's national security will be characterized by a people regathered from the nations in the latter years who:

- Are at peace,
- Living in unwalled villages,
- Dwelling securely,
- Living without the protection of walls, bars or gates, such as security checkpoints.

Additionally, the Jewish state's economy at that time will be blessed with:

- Plunder and booty,
- Acquired livestock and goods,
- An abundance of silver and gold.

Israel is not currently living at peace, but is under constant threat of attack from Iran, Syria, Hezbollah, Hamas and others. Also, the Jewish state has a four-hundred-mile partition wall in the heartland that separates Palestinian terrorists from Israel proper. Moreover, Israel has walls on its northern border between Lebanon, southern border between Egypt, eastern border between Jordan and western border between the Gaza Strip. Additionally, there are security checkpoints inside the country. In fact Israel is the most fenced-in and fortified nation in the Middle East, and maybe in the world.

Below are a few headlines that point out Israel is not living without walls, bars or gates.

"Israel completes Lebanon border wall around Metulla" – 6/12/12, Times of Israel.

"Israel resumes construction of wall along Lebanon border" – 4/10/18, Middle East Monitor.

"Israel starts massive fence on southern border with Jordan" – 1/20/16, Times of Israel.

"Israel's border fence with Egypt has transformed the south" – 1/15/19, Jewish Journal.

"Israel announces completion of security barrier around Gaza" – 12/8/21, Defense News.

"Israel expands West Bank security fence as violence escalates in Jenin" – 8/3/22, Al-Monitor.

Ezekiel 28:24-26, which has already been quoted in this book, informs that Israel will not be able to dwell securely until judgments are executed upon their evil Arab neighbors "around them who despise them."

> "And they will dwell safely there, build houses, and plant vineyards; yes, they will dwell securely, when I execute judgments on all those around them who despise them. Then they shall know that I *am* the Lord their God."
> (Ezekiel 28:26)

Ezekiel 38:10-13 informs us that Russia's leader prepares an evil plan to invade Israel and capture great plunder. The plunder consists of the agricultural and commercial goods, as well as gold and silver identified above, but it will likely also include the natural gas supplies that Israel has recently discovered, developed and is now utilizing and exporting. Refer to the headline below.

"EU, Israel and Egypt sign deal to boost East Med gas exports to Europe" (6/15/22 - Reuters).

These verses also introduce four more populations into the prophecy, apparently as protestors. These are *Sheba* (Yemen), *Dedan* (Saudi Arabia), *the Merchants of Tarshish*, (Britain or Spain, or both), and *all their Young Lions*. (United States of America, and / or Central and South America). In my *NOW Prophecies* book, I present the biblical, historical, archaeological, geographical and geo-political case that Tarshish is the UK and the young lions includes the USA.

Thus, there are fifteen total participants in the Ezekiel 38 prophecy.

1. *God the Victor.* (Ezek. 38:14-39:6),
2. *Israel the intended victim,* but resultant benefactor. (Ezek. 38:10-13),
3. *The nine Magog invaders,* of Magog, Rosh, Meshech, Tubal, Persia, Ethiopia, Libya, Gomer and Togarmah. (Ezek. 38:1-6),
4. *The four protestors* of Sheba, Dedan, Tarshish and their Young Lions. (Ezek. 38:13).

God the Victor of Ezekiel 38

Ezekiel 38:14 through 39:6 informs us the attackers will be many, and they come against Israel primarily from the north. We are again reminded the event finds fulfillment in the "latter days," and that the Lord warned of the event well in advance. Moreover, these verses confirm that the invaders are destroyed by the Lord, through an Old Testament type of fire and brimstone battle. This is important to note, because it reminds us that neither the Israel Defense Forces (IDF) nor the American troops are involved in this battle.

The sequence of supernatural war events are:

1. A great earthquake in Israel. (Ezek. 38:19),
2. The invaders, who speak differing languages, will panic from the results of the great earthquake and start killing one another. (Ezek. 38:21),
3. Pestilence and bloodshed, flooding rains, great hailstones, fire and brimstone. (Ezek. 38:22).

Ezekiel 39:7-8 provides the Lord's purpose for personally defeating this massive Mideast invasion. This verse was quoted earlier in this chapter.

> "So I will make My holy name known in the midst of My people Israel, and I will not *let them* profane My holy name anymore. Then the nations shall know that *I am* the LORD, the Holy One in Israel. Surely it is coming, and it shall be done," says the Lord GOD. "This *is* the day of which I have spoken."
> (Ezekiel 39:7-9)

This above passage requires that "*My people Israel*," the Jews, exist and that they possess the Promised Land, "*in Israel.*" This means that Hitler could not have completely exterminated the Jews in WWII, and that the Arab confederacy could not wipe Israel off of the map and take over the land of Israel in Psalm 83:12.

Moreover, "*My people Israel*," are the Chosen People and "*in Israel*" is in the Promised Land. These are two key components of the Abrahamic Covenant. By defending the Chosen People and preserving the Promised Land, the LORD proves that He keeps His unconditional covenant with Abraham.

Ezekiel 39:9-10 clues us in to the types of weaponry the invaders possess. Israel will be able to convert the enemy weapons into fuel for at least seven years. The picture is of energy provision for the entire nation, rather than a few isolated households. Ezekiel 39:9 says, "those who dwell in the cities," utilize these converted weapons for fuel.

The widespread use and lengthy seven-year span suggests that the weapons must be far more sophisticated than wooden bows and arrows, which would undoubtedly only last a short while. I mention this because some expositors today limit the weapons to wooden ones. I doubt nuclear non-proliferation will reduce Russian arsenals to wood between now and then.

There may actually be more than seven years' worth of fuel provided by these weapons, but the possibility looms large that the events occurring at the mid-point of the Tribulation Period interrupt the continued usage of the weapons. At this critical *mid-tribulation* point on the end times timeline, three-and-one-half years into the Tribulation Period, Israelis come under genocidal attack by the Antichrist. Thus, they are preoccupied with survival and probably not weapons conversion. If so, then there could be eight-plus years of weapons fuel, but no Jews taking time to harness the additional energy.

These missiles and rockets probably include the ABCs of weaponry—atomic, biological, and chemical. We can presume this because these types of weapons already exist inside the arsenals of Russia and some of their cohorts. Additionally, the dead soldiers appear to require Hazmat (Hazardous Materials) teams to assist with their burial according to Ezekiel 39:14-16. The fascinating fact is that whatever the weapons configuration, Israel will possess the technological know-how to convert them into national energy. Today, whether it is cell phones or irrigation techniques, Israel is on the cutting edge of technological advances.

Presently, nuclear weapons can be converted into a source of energy. America has been using this technology for years. See the headlines below.

"Megatons To Megawatts: Russian Warheads Fuel U.S. Power Plants" (12/11/13 – NPR).

"Power For US From Russia's Old Nuclear Weapons" (9/9/09 – NY Times).

"Russian nuclear warheads provided electricity for the US for 20 years" (3/8/21 –We are the Mighty).

Ezekiel 39:11-16 describes the location of the mass burial grounds of the destroyed armies of Gog. A valley east of what is probably the Dead Sea is renamed the Valley of Hamon Gog, which means the "hordes or multitudes" of Gog, in Hebrew. This would place the possible location of this massive graveyard in Central Jordan, which Israel should possess by then as per the fulfillment of Zephaniah 2:8-9. Israel's annexation of Jordan was pointed out in the previous chapter entitled, "The Psalm 83 Peripheral War Prophecies."

In this section, we also find that the Israelis will be burying the dead in order to cleanse the land. This could imply two things. One, that the hordes of Gog's dead soldiers are contaminated, requiring a professional quarantined burial and two, that the Jews are adhering to their ancient Levitical Law. Concerning the latter, Dr. Ron Rhodes writes in his book *Northern Storm Rising*:

"From the perspective of the Jews, the dead must be buried because exposed corpses are a source of ritual contamination to the land (Numbers 19:11-22; Deuteronomy 21:1-9). The land must therefore be completely cleansed and purged of all defilement. Neither the enemies nor their belongings (their weapons) can be left to pollute the land!"[40]

Ezekiel 39:17-20 is an invitation *"to every sort of bird and to every beast of the field"* to partake of the sacrificial meal of the "flesh" and "blood" of the invaders. Additionally foretold, the creatures are instructed to, *"eat the flesh of the mighty"* and *"drink the blood of the princes."*

One telltale sign that Ezekiel 39:17-20 is soon to happen is the fact that these birds of prey are already settling in mass in Israel. The logic is that when the birds gather for the sacrificial meal of the slain Magog invaders, they can't migrate from faraway places, but must already be on location. Below are a few headlines that illustrate that these birds are already nesting in Israel.

"Egyptian vultures return to Carmel mountains after 60 years." (5/22/19 –Times of Israel).

> "Vulture thought extinct from Israel for 30 years spotted twice in a month." (5/6/21 – Times of Israel).
>
> "Israeli Vulture Population on the Rise." (1/24/17 – Jerusalem Post).
>
> "The Iraqi Bird(s) That Made Aliyah." (5/14/07 – Haaretz).
>
> "Why Israel is a pilgrimage site for birds." (1/26/16 – Times of Israel).
>
> "Israel's 500 Million Birds: The World's Eighth Wonder" (1/23/17 – Haaretz).

Ezekiel 39:21-29 concludes the chapter with a recap of some Jewish history and a promise to the faithful remnant of Israel that the Lord will pour out His spirit upon them in the end.

The Timing of Ezekiel 38-39

First and foremost, we are told in Ezekiel 38:8, 16 that this prophecy finds fulfillment in the latter years, which the signs of the times strongly suggest, is where mankind presently finds itself on the end times timeline.

Second, it appears to happen after the Psalm 83 prophecy and its peripheral wars have happened. This is probably why Israel will be dwelling securely as a peaceful people in unwalled villages without the need for border walls and security checkpoints.

Third, it probably finds fulfillment before the Seven Year Tribulation Period, because the LORD will likely seek to notify the nations that His name is Holy and that He's the Holy One in Israel before the Antichrist comes on the scene and competes for the worship of mankind. The Antichrist plays a dominant role during the Tribulation.

Fourth, it appears to find fulfillment at least three and one-half years before the Seven Year Tribulation Period because that will enable the Jews to convert the enemy weapons into fuel. The theory is that in the first three and one-half years of the Tribulation the Jews can work with these weapons, but in the second three and one-half years they won't be able to. This is because they will be fleeing from the Jewish genocidal campaign of the Antichrist in Zechariah 13:8 and elsewhere.

So, they could burn the weapons for three and one-half years prior to the Tribulation Period and they could continue this process in the first half when they live in a condition of peace. This initial peace is achieved when they sign the seven-year covenant in Daniel 9:27. However, this peace is shattered at the midpoint of the seven years.

14

The Wars of the Seal Judgments

This chapter covers the following topics:

- The Wars of the Antichrist as the *(White Horseman)*,
- The World Wars of the *(Fiery Red Horseman)*,
- The War-torn World of the *(Black Horseman)*,
- The First Future Holy War of the *(Pale Horsemen)*,
- The First Holy War Victims are the *(Fifth Seal Saints)*.

Following the sequence of prophetic wars as outlined thus far in this book, the next battles are described in the Seal Judgments of Revelation 6. Probably happening shortly after the Ezekiel 38 war, the four horsemen of the apocalypse come galloping on to the world stage.

The Wars of the Antichrist as the (White Horseman)

First Seal: The Conqueror

> "Now I saw when the Lamb opened one of the seals; and I heard one of the four living creatures saying with a voice like thunder, "Come and see." And I looked, and behold, a white horse. He who sat on it had a bow; and a crown was given to him, and he went out conquering and to conquer."
> (Revelation 6:1-2)

The rider on the "white horse" is commonly taught to be the Antichrist. When he comes on the scene he embarks upon a threefold campaign below.

1. He will become a world political leader who:
   a. Israel trusts to confirm a covenant on its behalf, (Daniel 9:27).
   b. The Harlot relies upon to emerge as the global religion, (Rev. 17:3, 7).
   c. Ten Kings will align with in a global government, (Rev. 17:12).
2. He will become a military leader who is winning wars, (Daniel 11:40-45).
3. He emerges as the world's supreem religious leader, (Revelation 13:3, 15).

As he goes about his business of "conquering and to conquer" with his bow in hand and crown on his head, he will prevail politically, overcome militarily and overpower religiously, which happens at the midpoint of the Tribulation Period. He will become victorious in these three important arenas.

Daniel 11:40, informs that the Antichrist will enter into the countries of the king of the South and the king of the North and overwhelm them, and pass through.

Daniel 11:41 predicts that he will then enter into the "glorious land," which likely represents significant portions of the Middle East, and he will overthrow many countries with the exception of Jordan.

Daniel 11:42-44 follows his warpath into Egypt. He will conquer Egypt and capture its "treasures of gold and silver," and also "the Libyans and Ethiopians shall follow at his heels."

This conquest of Egypt likely fulfills the prophecies in Ezekiel 29:12, which leads to forty years of desolation of Egypt and forty years of Egyptian dispersion.

> "I will make the land of Egypt desolate in the midst of the countries that are desolate; and among the cities that are laid waste, her cities shall be desolate forty years; and I will scatter the Egyptians among the nations and disperse them throughout the countries."
> (Ezekiel 29:12)

The World Wars of the (Fiery Red Horseman)

> "When He opened the second seal, I heard the second living creature saying, "Come and see." Another horse, fiery red, went out. And it was granted to the one who sat on it to take peace from the earth, and that people should kill one another; and there was given to him a great sword."
> (Revelation 6:3-4)

The rider on the fiery red horse is wielding a "great sword." In the Bible a sword can be either a literal sword or a typology for war. In this passage it represents widespread war that takes *"peace from the earth, and that people should kill one another."* Thus, it appears to foretell the coming of a future world war.

We are not informed of what nations are specifically involved, but the fact that the whole earth is adversely affected, it could be a world war on a nuclear scale. Perhaps it could include scenarios such as, China vs. Taiwan, India vs. Pakistan or N. Korea vs. S. Korea. It could also include the Ezekiel 38 war if that hadn't happened prior.

The War-torn World of the (Black Horseman)

> "When He opened the third seal, I heard the third living creature say, "Come and see." So I looked, and behold, a black horse, and he who sat on it had a

pair of scales in his hand. And I heard a voice in the midst of the four living creatures saying, "A quart of wheat for a denarius, and three quarts of barley for a denarius; and do not harm the oil and the wine." (Revelation 6:5-6)

The introduction of the Black Horseman signifies that the darkest of times have fallen upon the earth. When great wars happen, severe suffering results. Famines occur as plagues and pestilences spread uncontrollably throughout the war zones. This creates a humanitarian crisis as refugees surface and become stranded in the affected areas. The fact that the prior horseman wielded a great sword, implies that the global consequences of the second seal wars were catastrophic.

The third seal imposes the enormous burden upon the international community to resolve the disastrous dilemma before it burgeons out of control. It encourages the expeditious formation of a global government to deal with the escalating emergencies, such as world starvation and disease control. It appears from the details in Revelation 6:7-8, that the fourth and following horsemen of the Pale Horse will be tasked with restoring order around the globe.

Be it the Pale Horse, or whoever takes responsibility for administering aid to the afflicted, the Black Horseman instructs them to ration the world's food supplies. The price tag for the necessary food staples to survive becomes fixed at two days' wages. A denarius was the equivalent of a day's wage when this prophecy was written. One denarius will put a quart of wheat inside a family's gallon container and another denarius will fill the remainder of their vessel with three quarts of barley.

The third seal paints a grave picture for the poor, but it's not as distressing for the rich. The horseman concludes his instructions with the command, *"do not harm the oil and the wine."* This alludes to the luxury items that only the rich will be able to afford. In other words, in the process of rationing the food, do not harm the economic engine that drives the financial recovery, which sustains the existence of the global government.

The First Future Holy War of the (Pale Horsemen)

As the title implies there are future Holy wars coming. There are at least two, which are perpetrated by first, the Harlot World Religion and second, the Antichrist. The Pale Horse war may represent a third holy war, but more than likely is related to the Christian killing crusade of the Harlot in Revelation 17:6.

> "When He opened the fourth seal, I heard the voice of the fourth living creature saying, "Come and see." So I looked, and behold, a pale horse. And the name of him who sat on it was Death, and Hades followed with him. And power was given to them over a fourth of the earth, to kill with sword, with hunger, with death, and by the beasts of the earth."
> (Revelation 6:7-8)

[Handwritten margin note: World Population 8.1 Billion]

As the seals progress in their chronological order, things go from bad to worse as the world welcomes in the Pale Horsemen of the Apocalypse. I say horsemen, rather than horseman, because unlike its three predecessors the Pale horse has two riders. This sinister tag team rides side saddle in their natural order, Death followed by Hades.

Death deals with the material departure of a being from its body and Hades is concerned with the immaterial aspect of a person after death, which is their soul. Presently, when someone dies their soul is delivered to its destination, which is either Heaven if they're saved or Hades if they're not. Thus, it appears that the Pale Horse has spiritual connotations and could represent the Harlot World Religion of Mystery Babylon of Revelation 17. I argue this case in my book entitled, *The NEXT Prophecies*.

You can read my reasons for making this connection online as part of my thesis called, "*The Post Rapture / Pre-Tribulation Gap Thesis.*" It's available at this weblink, http://www.prophecydepotministries.net/wordpress/wp-content/uploads/2017/05/APOC-ROAD-FINAL-THESIS.pdf

Whoever, or whatever the Pale Horsemen represent, this diabolical duo seemingly possesses power and authority over a quarter of the world's population to kill people via multiple means. Unlike the second horseman who only had a great sword in his sheath, Death and Hades have a lethal arsenal that enables them to kill with sword, with hunger, with death, and by the beasts of the earth.

The traditional teaching is that Death and Hades kill a fourth of mankind, but that's not necessarily what's being said here. Compare the differences in language between the fourth seal and the sixth trumpet in the book of Revelation.

> "By these three plagues (of the sixth trumpet) a third of mankind was killed—by the fire and the smoke and the brimstone which came out of their mouths."
> (Rev. 9:18 NKJV; emphasis added)

This above verse clearly states that a third of mankind was killed by the three plagues that followed the sounding of the sixth trumpet. However, Revelation 6:8 says, "And power was given to them over a fourth of the earth, to kill with sword, with hunger, with death, and by the beasts of the earth." The New American Standard Bible translates this verse to read, "Authority was given to them over a fourth of the earth, to kill with sword and with famine and with pestilence and by the wild beasts of the earth."

Let's unpack this further. *"Authority was given to them over a fourth of the earth..."*

At a time when the world is recovering from devastating wars, severe famines and enormous economic scarcities, Death and Hades ride onto the scene. It appears that these two riders come to the rescue and harness global control over one-fourth of the world's surviving population. Some Bible prophecy experts suggest that a fourth of the earth at that time could be approximately two billion people.

If Death and Hades are called to restore order amidst the global chaos, then a global reach of two billion people would seem adequate to enable them to execute their campaign successfully. It is likely that many of the other six billion, (three-fourths of the earth), survivors are suffering from the consequences of the wars and famines. Perhaps Death and Hades command their global network of about two billion to remedy the dire conditions occurring throughout the world.

However, for the benefit of receiving assistance from the global network of Death and Hades, the needy must follow their dictates. Those who dissent are put to death by either, "the sword and with famine and with pestilence and by the wild beasts of the earth." This becomes evident in the prophetic text of the following Fifth Seal, which is included at the close of this chapter.

It may mean that Death and Hades kill a fourth of the earth's population, which is what the traditional view teaches, but more than likely it implies that a quarter of the world's population are faithful followers of Death and Hades. These are devotees so committed to their cause that they are willing to kill their opposition.

The fact that Hades takes a lead role in this massive operation infers that this involves a global religious crusade. This future scenario appears to be reminiscent of the historical inquisition periods when the Catholic Church was martyring the so-called Protestant heretics centuries ago.

The First Holy War Victims are the (Fifth Seal Saints)

> "When He opened the fifth seal, I saw under the altar the souls of those who had been slain for the word of God and for the testimony which they held. And they cried with a loud voice, saying, "How long, O Lord, holy and true, until You judge and avenge our blood on those who dwell on the earth?" Then a white robe was given to each of them; and it was said to them that they should rest a little while longer, until both

the number of their fellow servants and their brethren, who would be killed as they *were*, was completed." (Revelation 6:9-11)

Lo and behold, Death and Hades are killing believers for professing the word of God and living out their Christian testimony. True Christian believers may not be the only group they are killing, but they are at least one of them.

This means that Death and Hades must be perpetrating a spiritual message that runs contrary to the gospel of Jesus Christ. The Fifth Seal Saints will hold fast, even to the point of death, to the biblical narrative, which is that Jesus Christ is the way, the truth and the life and the only means of salvation as per John 14:6.

This message of the Fifth Seal Saints must be antithetical to the teachings of Death and Hades. As such, the quarter of the world's population that adheres to the religious view presented by Death and Hades, is called upon to martyr these Christian dissenters. The slaying of an untold number of Christians implies that the killing campaign of Death and Hades, is not religiously tolerant! Apparently, Death and Hades will not be propagating an ecumenical message, such as "*all roads lead to heaven.*"

The Fifth Seal Saints represent one of three groups that are martyred for their Christian beliefs. Revelation 6:11 groups them as the Fifth Seal Saints, their fellow servants and the brethren of the fellow servants. My thesis mentioned prior in this chapter, explains who these groups appear to represent. Below is an excerpt from the thesis.

"The Fifth Seal Saints ask the LORD a telling question. "*How long, O Lord, holy and true, until You judge and avenge our blood on those who dwell on the earth?*" God's response to their question is interesting. He sums up the metric of time by identifying their Christian condition.

The LORD replies, that Christ will return in the Second Coming, which is the time that their blood will be avenged, when the full number of believers who are martyred for their faith is complete. He identifies the three phases of Christian martyrdom for them.

> "Then a white robe was given to each of them; (Group 1) and it was said to them that they should rest a little while longer, until both the number of "their fellow servants" (Group 2) and "their brethren," (Group 3) who would be killed as they were, was completed."
> (Rev. 6:11; emphasis added)

The three phases of Christian martyrdom after the Rapture apparently break down in the manner described below.

1. The Post-Rapture / Pre-Trib gap period: (Group 1) - This phase is when the Fifth Seal Saints are slain. It has previously been established in this thesis, that they are killed by Death and Hades. They are likely among those killed by the Harlot, who is "the woman" in Revelation 17:6, who is "drunk with the blood of the saints and with the blood of the martyrs of Jesus."

2. The first half of the Tribulation Period: (Group 2) - The second phase involves the "fellow servants" of the Fifth Seal Saints. They are killed during the first half of the Tribulation Period by the same executioner as the Fifth Seal Saints. The Harlot is drunk with their blood also. The fact that they are martyred by the same hands appropriately classifies them as fellow servants with the Fifth Seal Saints.

3. The second half of the Tribulation Period: (Group 3) - The final phase of martyrdom involves the "brethren" of the fellow servants who previously died in the second phase. By the time the brethren are martyred, the Harlot will have been desolated by the ten kings in Rev. 17:16. This means the brethren are killed by a different source. The brethren are beheaded by the Antichrist for refusing to worship him

by taking his "Mark of the Beast." The fact that they die during the Tribulation Period adequately connects the *fellow servants*, who also died in the Tribulation Period, with their *brethren*."

(Refer to the image below). Please note that the identification of these three groups is the author's exclusive interpretation, so do your own research to see if you agree.

3 Periods of Post-Rapture Christian Martyrdom

	False Covenant Confirmed		Ten Kings Desolate Harlot	
Harlot Kills 5th Seal Saints		**Harlot Kills Fellow Servants** of 5th Seal Saints		**Antichrist Beheads Brethren** of Fellow Servants
Post-Rapture Pre-Trib Time-Gap *"How Long oh Lord?"*		First three and one-half years 1260 Days	Midpoint	Second three and one-half years 1260 Days

15

The Wars of the Trumpet Judgments

This chapter covers the following topics:

- The Locust War of Torment of the Fifth Trumpet in Revelation 9:1-11,
- The War of the Sixth Trumpet that kills one-third of mankind in Revelation 9:12-21.

Following the wars of the first four Seal Judgments, the next major battles are described in the Fifth and Sixth Trumpet Judgments of Revelation 9. Unlike the wars described in the Seals, which were primarily perpetrated by evil men, the Trumpet wars are seemingly carried out by demons and angels. In my book entitled, *The Last Prophecies, the Prophecies in the First 3 ½ Years of the Tribulation*, I point out that these two wars happen in the first 3 ½ years of the Tribulation Period.

Before exploring these two Trumpet Judgment wars it's important to note that they represent two of the three "*Woe Judgments*" in the book of Revelation. They are appropriately labeled as "*Woe Judgments*" because they are the most severe of the twenty-one judgments of Revelation contained within the Seven Seals, Seven Trumpets and Seven Bowls.

"And I looked, and I heard an angel flying through
the midst of heaven, saying with a loud voice,
"Woe, woe, woe to the inhabitants of the earth,
because of the remaining blasts of the trumpet

of the three angels who are about to sound!'"
(Rev. 8:13)

Woe #1 is the Fifth Trumpet. Woe #2 is the Sixth Trumpet. Woe #3 is the Seventh Trumpet, which unleashes the Seven Bowl Judgments of Revelation chapter 16. According to Revelation 15:1, the wrath of God is completed in Woe #3 through the Seven Bowl Judgments.

The Locust War of Torment of the Fifth Trumpet in Revelation 9:1-11

This future battle is unique in the history of warfare because it is:

- Fought by demons, in the author's estimation, against humans,
- Purposed to torment people, rather than kill them,
- Happening within a prescribed time frame of only five months,
- Waged only against unsaved people who are alive in the first 3 ½ years of the Tribulation Period.

"Then the fifth angel sounded: And I saw a star fallen from heaven to the earth. To him was given the key to the bottomless pit. And he opened the bottomless pit, and smoke arose out of the pit like the smoke of a great furnace. So the sun and the air were darkened because of the smoke of the pit. Then out of the smoke locusts came upon the earth. And to them was given power, as the scorpions of the earth have power. They were commanded not to harm the grass of the earth, or any green thing, or any tree, but only those men who do not have the seal of God on their foreheads. And they were not given authority to kill them, but to torment them for five months. Their torment was like the torment of a scorpion when it strikes a man.

> In those days men will seek death and will not find it;
> they will desire to die, and death will flee from them."
> (Rev. 9:1-6)

This above passage informs that a fallen star from heaven comes to the earth on a mission. We are told in Rev. 9:11, that this star is a fallen angel named "*in Hebrew is Abaddon, but in Greek he has the name Apollyon,*" which means "destroyer." We are also informed in this verse that these locusts, "*had as king over them* (this) *angel of the bottomless pit.*"

Locusts or Demonic Beings?

Some, including myself, believe that these locusts are actually demonic beings. Below is a quote from John Walvoord.

> "These locusts, however, did not eat vegetation, but had the power to torment people for five months. Thus they might be demons who appeared in the form of locusts. This is confirmed by the fact that they came from the abyss, the home of demons (Luke 8:31)."[41]

In Rev. 3-6, we receive solid clues that these are not garden-variety locusts, but are demonic beings.

1. *They originate from the Bottomless Pit* – This is not where locusts come from. Locusts go through egg, nymph and adult stages -- lacking the pupa stage. This means that actual locusts are birthed on the earth, whereas these demon locusts come from the Bottomless Pit. Luke 8:31 points out that the abode of demons is the abyss, which is the same as the Bottomless Pit.
2. *They have power like scorpions to strike men* – Locusts don't even bite people, let alone sting or strike them like a scorpion.

3. *They follow instructions not to "harm the grass of the earth, or any green thing, or any tree* – since locusts feed upon foliage and stems of plants such as herbs and grasses, it's not reasonable to assume they will ignore these fine locust delicacies.
4. *They have spiritual discernment* – they are instructed to torment only those men who do not have the Seal of God on their foreheads. The Seal of God distinguishes the saved from the unsaved, and is not likely a visible marking on a person's forehead.

At this juncture of time, the saved people are not going to banner their salvation visibly with a seal stamped on their forehead because the Harlot World Religion will easily spot them and martyr them as per Rev. 17:6. However, in Rev. 13:16, after this locust judgment is fully completed, the False Prophet will initiate the Mark of the Beast, which will place a visible mark on the right hand or forehead of the unsaved, but that's an unrelated event. Therefore, these strange locusts most likely act more like demonic beings possessing the spiritual knowledge of who is unsaved and fair game to torment, rather than mere large insects.

5. *They don't know how to read a calendar* – these locusts operate within a defined window of time. They are only tormenting unsaved people for five months. Unlike demonic beings, locusts don't know how to tell time. In fact the average lifespan of an adult locust is between 8 to 10 weeks, which means that if these were truly locusts, most of them would die off midway during their five-month mission.[42]
6. *They can't determine when too much torment leads to death* – These locusts are only to torment, not kill the unsaved. A locust would not know when to stop tormenting a person, but a demonic being would.

7. *These locusts don't look like actual locusts* – The next passage further disqualifies these locusts as literal locusts and further identifies them as demonic beings.

"The shape of the locusts was like horses prepared for battle. On their heads were crowns of something like gold, and their faces were like the faces of men. They had hair like women's hair, and their teeth were like lions' teeth. And they had breastplates like breastplates of iron, and the sound of their wings was like the sound of chariots with many horses running into battle. They had tails like scorpions, and there were stings in their tails. Their power was to hurt men five months. And they had as king over them the angel of the bottomless pit, whose name in Hebrew is Abaddon, but in Greek he has the name Apollyon."
(Rev. 9:7-11)

These five verses provide us with more details into the identity and purpose of the locust invaders. These details enumerated below set them apart figuratively as demonic beings, rather than literally as insects. These locusts of the Fifth Trumpet Judgment in no way resemble real locusts because:

a. They are shaped like horses prepared for battle,
b. On their heads were crowns of something like gold,
c. Their faces were like the faces of men,
d. They had hair like women's hair,
e. Their teeth were like lions' teeth,
f. They had breastplates like breastplates of iron,
g. The sound of their wings was like the sound of chariots.
h. They are ruled by a fallen angel named "Apollyon," demons have fallen angel friends, but not locusts.

Are the Locusts A.I. Drones or Robots?

It's obvious that these are not real locust insects, but are they actually demonic beings from the Bottomless Pit, or could they possibly be A.I. Drones or Robots? There is a relatively new theory being floated in a few prophetic circles that the locusts of the Fifth Trumpet Judgment may be drones or robots programmed with Artificial Intelligence (A.I.).

One of the prophetic details that some believe identifies drones in the Fifth Trumpet Judgment is found in the verse below.

> "And they, (the locusts) had breastplates like breastplates of iron, and the sound of their wings was like the sound of chariots with many horses running into battle."
> (Rev. 9:9; emphasis added)

If this was the only detail about these locusts, then their idea could have credibility. However, there are many other details scattered through Rev. 9:1-11, some that were just listed, that I believe mitigate against this possibility. Some of the problems with this teaching are below.

- The majority of breastplates for human soldiers have been made of bronze or iron for centuries. Thus, this is not a new or unique detail that can only now be attributed to A.I. robots.
- The Locusts originate from the smoke that comes out of the Bottomless Pit, rather than a Robot manufacturing factory somewhere. (Rev. 9:2-3)
- The commander of these locusts is the fallen angel named Apollyon rather than an A.I. programming specialist. (Rev. 9:11)
- The Locusts only torment men for five months, which poses the question: "Will an A.I. robot know the limits between killing and tormenting someone?" One tormented person that dies at the hands of an A.I. robot seemingly nullifies

this entire theory. The pertinent verse is below. "In those days men will seek death and will not find it; they will desire to die, and death will flee from them." (Rev. 9:6) It is difficult to think that a robot or drone would know its limitations to be in compliance with this prophetic detail.

- Will a robot be able to determine who has the Seal of God? The locusts receive specific instructions in this verse. "*They were commanded not to harm the grass of the earth, or any green thing, or any tree, but only those men who do not have the seal of God on their foreheads.*" (Rev. 9:4; emphasis added) It would seem that determining who has the Seal of God would require spiritual rather than technological discernment. Such selectivity is something that apparently Apollyon possesses as the commander of the tormenting locusts. If the locusts are demonic beings, then they would also likely have the ability to decipher who to torment.

In light of all the above, "Woe #1" literally introduces demonic warfare into the end times equation. This is not symbolic, but actual high-ranking demonic beings capable of warring against mankind. This locust scenario sets the stage for two even more powerful angelic wars that follow, which are the war of "Woe #2" and the War in Heaven of Revelation 12:7-9.

How will the news media and governments of the world explain what or who is specifically attacking people worldwide at this future time? Will people recognize that these demonic creatures arise from the Bottomless Pit as part of God's judgment upon sinful mankind? This is not likely, but what if these attackers are falsely labeled as alien creatures from another planet, would that be a more realistic explanation?

It's interesting to note that the demonic entities are specifically targeting those who do not have the Seal of God. It appears as though the LORD is allowing this demonic attack to happen as a wake-up call for people to get saved and get the Seal of God. Thus, Woe #1 apparently serves as a powerful prompt to act for the unsaved person to get saved and escape the ongoing torment of these locust-like demonic creatures from the Bottomless Pit.

Below is a summary from the book of Ephesians on how to receive the Seal of God.

"In Him, (*Jesus Christ*), you, (*the believer*), also trusted, after you heard the word of truth, the gospel of your salvation; in whom also, having believed, you were sealed with the Holy Spirit of promise, who is the guarantee of our inheritance until the redemption of the purchased possession, to the praise of His glory."
(Ephesians 1:13-14; emphasis added)

These two Ephesians verses above emphasize the critical role of the gospel message of salvation in the process. The sequence of events are as follows:

1. A person hears the "word of truth," which is the gospel message of salvation,
2. They believe it,
3. Then they receive it; meaning they accept Jesus Christ as their Lord and Savior,
4. Having heard, believed and received, they put all of their trust "In Him," (Jesus Christ),
5. As a result of their decision to become a believer, they are sealed with the Holy Spirit,
6. The Holy Spirit serves as the spiritual guarantor of the believer's eternal redemption.

The War of the Sixth Trumpet that kills one-third of mankind in Revelation 9:12-21

> "One woe is past. Behold, still two more
> woes are coming after these things."
> (Rev. 9:12)

The first of the three woe judgments concludes with the completion of the five-month demonic locust invasion. This solo verse above provides a clear break in the action between the passing of Woe #1 and the comings of Woe #2 and Woe #3. It serves as the segue that introduces Woe #2, which finds fulfillment through the Sixth Trumpet Judgment.

Revelation 9:12 concludes with the two Greek words "*meta tauta,*" which *means hereafter, afterward, after this,* or *after these things.* This reinforces the fact that after the Fifth Trumpet Judgment the Sixth Trumpet Judgment ensues. These two Woe Judgments do not overlap, but happen in a sequence. This is also the case with Woe #3.

> "The second woe is past. Behold, the third woe is coming
> quickly."(Rev. 11:14)

After the Sixth Trumpet Judgment of Woe #2, Woe #3 follows quickly. Woe #3 unleashes the plagues contained in the Seven Bowl Judgments of Revelation 16, through which the wrath of God is completed.

> "Then I saw another sign in heaven, great and
> marvelous: seven angels having the seven last plagues, for
> in them the wrath of God is complete."
> (Rev. 15:1)

In my book entitled, T*he LAST Prophecies, the Prophecies in the First 3 ½ Years of the Tribulation*, I point out in the chapter called, "The Seven Trumpet Judgments," that the first two woes happen inthe first half of the Tribulation Period and Woe #3 happens in the second half of this period. (Refer to the image below).

Seven-Year Tribulation Period

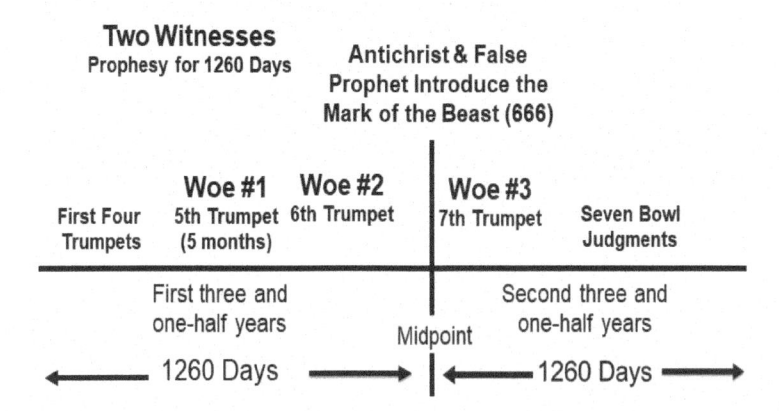

	Two Witnesses Prophesy for 1260 Days		**Antichrist & False Prophet Introduce the Mark of the Beast (666)**		
	Woe #1	**Woe #2**	**Woe #3**		
First Four Trumpets	5th Trumpet (5 months)	6th Trumpet	7th Trumpet	Seven Bowl Judgments	
	First three and one-half years		Second three and one-half years		
	←—— 1260 Days ——→	Midpoint	←—— 1260 Days ——→		

Woes #1 and #2 seemingly prime the unsaved population to receive the Antichrist as their world leader. When these first two woes conclude at the midpoint of the Seven Year Tribulation Period, the Antichrist and his cohort the False Prophet put forward their global campaign to reign supreme over the world, which includes the introduction of the Mark of the Beast in Rev. 13:16-17.

Woe #2, the Sixth Trumpet Judgment

> "Then the sixth angel sounded: And I heard a voice from the four horns of the golden altar which is before God, saying to the sixth angel who had the trumpet, "Release the four angels who are bound at the great river Euphrates." So the four angels, who had been prepared for the hour and day and month and year, were released to kill a third of mankind. Now the number of the army of the horsemen was two hundred million; I heard the number of them. And thus I saw the horses in the vision: those who sat on them had breastplates of fiery red, hyacinth blue, and sulfur yellow; and the heads of the horses were like the heads of lions; and out

of their mouths came fire, smoke, and brimstone. By these three plagues a third of mankind was killed—by the fire and the smoke and the brimstone which came out of their mouths. For their power is in their mouth and in their tails; for their tails are like serpents, having heads; and with them they do harm. But the rest of mankind, who were not killed by these plagues, did not repent of the works of their hands, that they should not worship demons, and idols of gold, silver, brass, stone, and wood, which can neither see nor hear nor walk. And they did not repent of their murders or their sorceries or their sexual immorality or their thefts."
(Rev. 9:13-21)

Woe #2 of the Sixth Trumpet Judgment involves five angels and 200-million mounted troops, which appears to be composed of demonic beings. One of the angels, the trumpeter is good, but the other four are bad, which is why they *"are bound at the great river Euphrates."* The fact that this vast army is led by four bad angels suggests that they are demonic beings rather than human beings. Below is a quote from John Walvoord about the demonic nature of these four angels.

"These four angels are clearly demons, as holy angels are not bound."[43]

Before the sounding of the Sixth Trumpet, four bad angels will be bound at the Euphrates River which courses through modern-day Syria and Iraq. They may already be bound there! Prior to their release, these angels prepare for a singular mission, which is not to spread good tidings of comfort and joy, but is to kill one-third of mankind! This could amount to well over a billion people at that time.

Who are these soldiers? Where do they come from? Are they killing people throughout the world, or only within the Middle East, which is the location of the Euphrates River? Are they killing believers or unbelievers, or both?

Who are these soldiers? Where do they come from?

Concerning the identity and origin of these soldiers, we are given clues in Rev. 9:17-19 from John's vision.

1. John saw horses with heads like lions and mouths that emitted fire, smoke and brimstone. These horses had tails like serpents having heads,
2. The apostle also saw horsemen riding these horses that were adorned with colorful breastplates of fiery red, hyacinth blue, and sulfur yellow.

Some believe that these horsemen represent the Chinese army for two primary reasons. *First*, the reference to the Euphrates River in Rev. 9:14 is also made in relationship to the "Kings of the East" in Rev. 16:12. They believe that the Kings of the East could allude to the Asian Kings of the Orient, which includes China.

Second, China once boasted that it could field an army of 200 million men.[44] Thus, the formula is: (Kings of the East + 200 million) = the Chinese Army.

Below are quotes from Dr. David Reagan and Dr. Andy Wood that suggest that these two hundred million horsemen could represent, or at least include, The People's Liberation Army of China (PLA), or in Wood's quote, an army from the Far East.

"Or consider the prophecy in Revelation 9 that an army of 200 million will march across Asia to Israel in the end times. When that prophecy was written, there were not even 200 million people on planet earth. Today, one nation, China, can send such an army."[45] (Dr. David Reagan)

"When you put Revelation 9 verse 14 and you study with Revelation 16 verse 12 those are the sixth trumpet and bowl judgments and basically what they're talking about is this giant army from the Far East. It looks like it numbers 200 million. It's

> *going to make its way from the Far East towards Northern Israel to participate in the final battle called the battle of Armageddon. The Euphrates river is supernaturally dried up to expedite the path and along the way they kill a third of mankind which is stunning... So this is a giant army that's moving towards Northern Israel."*[46] (Dr. Andy Woods)

Both Reagan and Woods suggest that the army is comprised of human beings rather than demonic beings. They also teach that this vast army is marching to Israel, which implies that the slaughtering of one-third of mankind is occurring primarily in the Middle East.

Below are at least three potential problems with this theory:

1. The reference to the Euphrates River in Rev. 16:12 alludes to the Sixth Bowl Judgment and is unrelated to the Sixth Trumpet Judgment. The Kings of the East who take part in the Sixth Bowl Judgment are not mentioned in the Sixth Trumpet Judgment.

Connecting the Kings of the East with the 200-million-man army by mere association with the Euphrates would be like linking the Chicago Bears with the Chicago Cubs because they both play in Chicago. No, they are two distinct teams, that play two entirely different sports and they perform during separate seasons. Similarly, the Sixth Trumpet and the Sixth Bowl are two different judgments that occur at separate times.

2. The Chinese Army doesn't resemble the descriptions of these horses and horsemen. I like what Dr. Arnold Fruchtenbaum says along these lines.

> "*A person would be hard pressed to find just one Chinese person who looks like this, let alone two hundred million of them. The description given of the army clearly rules out their being human and requires that they be demonic. Furthermore, the means by which the destruction of one-third of the world's population is accomplished (fire, smoke, brimstone), involves the supernatural rather than the natural.*"[47]

Another quote along these lines is included below from Dr. Ron Rhodes.

> "*In Revelation 9:16(ASV) we read of a large army in which the number of the armies of the horseman was twice ten thousand times ten thousand* " *(which is 200 million). Through the years there have been many who have assumed this must refer to the army of China, since China has long claimed to be able to mount an army of 200 million. Contextually, however, this does not seem to make sense. These 200 million are said to be led by four fallen angels(Revelation 9:14 -15). Besides, the description of these" mounted troops" appear to be anything but human in verse 17. Apparently, these are demonic spirits who, under the leadership of four fallen angels, bring about mass murder among humans, (see verses 15 and 18).*"[48]

3. The People's Liberation Army of China presently has a force of only about two million, not two hundred million. Below are some quotes from a Congressional Research Report published on June 4, 2021.[49]

> "*Overview of the PLA:*
>
> *A force of approximately two million men and women, the PLA is divided into four services: the PLA Army, PLA Navy, PLA Air Force, and the PLA Rocket Force, as well as two sub-service forces, the Strategic Support Force (which is responsible for cyber, electronic, information, and space and counterspace operations), and the Joint Logistics Support Force....the PLA has shrunk significantly from its estimated size of 5 million troops in 1949, to 3 million in 1992, to about 2 million active personnel today.*"

Another thing to consider is, the logistic difficulties of manifesting a two hundred million human army from China, or even an international force for that matter, seems impractical, nearly impossible and could take years to assemble. Recruiting, training, housing, deploying, feeding and arming an army of this magnitude has never been done before.

Are they killing people throughout the world, or only within the Middle East?

This is another valid question. What world populations are being affected by the Sixth Trumpet Judgment? Is this a global killing campaign, or does it only affect the peoples residing within the Mideast countries closest to the Euphrates River? I believe this is a worldwide war against all of mankind rather than just the Arabs, Jews and Persians of the Middle East.

Additionally, one-third of mankind is a much larger population than what exists in the Mideast. As of 2023 there are approximately 483,004,121[50] people in the Middle East, which represents only about 6% of mankind and not 33%! Understandably, the Sixth Trumpet Judgment is a future event, but it's not likely going to change these population percentage demographics by much. If anything, after the wars of Psalm 83 and Ezekiel 38, there should be a lesser percentage of the world's overall population dwelling in the Mideast.

I believe the Kings of the East of the Sixth Bowl Judgment are marching toward Israel, but by the time they deploy, the Sixth Trumpet Judgment will have already happened and one-third of mankind will have been killed by the 200 million demonic horsemen of Revelation 9:13-21.

Are they killing believers or unbelievers, or both?

Only unbelievers were tormented for five months in Woe #1, but does that remain true for Woe #2? The clues in Rev. 9:20-21 seem to suggest that believers are also protected from the killings in Woe #2.

These two verses state that the two-thirds of mankind who were not killed by the plagues of smoke, fire and brimstone did not repent from their works, or their worship of demons and idols. *"And they did not repent of their murders or their sorceries or their sexual immorality or their thefts."*

This leads me to conclude that believers are spared from both the Fifth and Sixth Trumpet Judgment killings. Believers have repentant hearts, but these survivors above do not. However, just because believers might escape death at the hands of the two hundred million demons, that doesn't mean they will not be distressed by the fire, smoke and brimstone. These types of plagues will undoubtedly create harsh living conditions in the affected territories.

Lastly, Joel 1:15-2:11 seems to give further details about the demonic invasions of Woe #1 and Woe #2. These verses describe the extremely harsh conditions that result from these invasions. There will be:

- Barns broken down, which results in withered grain (Joel 1:17),
- Restless cattle because there are no more pastures (Joel 1:18),
- Dry brooks and pastures burned by fire (Joel 1:20),
- People severely trembling, which could include believers (Joel 2:1),
- Atmospheric darkness and gloominess (Joel 2:2),
- Wildfires that turn places into desolate wastelands (Joel 2:3),
- People writhing in pain and pale in skin color (Joel 2:6),

- Well organized demonic armies that do not break their ranks, march in columns, run to and from within cities and break into houses like thieves to torment and kill people (Joel 2:7-9).

Conclusion

The Fifth and Sixth Trumpet Judgments introduce a new dimension of world warfare. This is because they seemingly pin fallen angels and their demonic being cohorts against mankind. The LORD does not prevent these wars from happening, but appears to protect believers from the torment of the demonic locust invasion of Woe #1 and the killings of the two hundred million demonic horsemen of Woe #2. These two wars redefine spiritual warfare and set the stage for the final few wars that follow.

16

The War in Heaven

"So it will happen on that day, That the Lord will punish the rebellious angels of heaven on high, And the kings of the earth on earth."
(Isaiah 24:21, NASB)

The prophet Isaiah informs that a time is coming when the LORD will punish Satan and his army of fallen angels. This chapter explains when, why and how this punishment will happen. Let's start by exploring the details of this war in heaven prophecy.

The Details of the War in Heaven (Revelation 12:7-12)

"And war broke out in heaven: Michael and his angels fought with the dragon; and the dragon and his angels fought, but they did not prevail, nor was a place found for them in heaven any longer. So the great dragon was cast out, that serpent of old, called the Devil and Satan, who deceives the whole world; he was cast to the earth, and his angels were cast out with him. Then I heard a loud voice saying in heaven, "Now salvation, and strength, and the kingdom of our God, and the power of His Christ have come, for the accuser of our brethren, who accused them before our God day and night, has been cast down. And they overcame him by the blood of the Lamb and by the word of their testimony, and they did not love their lives to the death. Therefore rejoice, O heavens, and you who dwell in them! Woe to the inhabitants of the earth and the sea! For the devil has come down to you, having great wrath, because he knows that he has a short time.'" (Rev. 12:7-12)

This is the war that serves as the punishment of Satan and the rebellious angels according to Isaiah 24:21 above. As a result of this war, Satan and his fallen angelic followers are cast down to earth. This future event relocates Satan into his fourth of seven abodes.

The Seven Abodes of Satan

The Bible tells us that Satan, at various points of his career, occupies seven separate addresses.

1. The First Abode: The Throne of God.
2. The Second Abode: The Mineral Garden of Eden.

The first two abodes are to be found in Ezekiel 28:11-15.

3. The Third Abode: The Atmospheric Heavens – (Ephesians 2:2 and 6:12). Presently, the Devil and his rebellious angels share dual citizenship between earth and heaven.
4. The Fourth Abode: The Earth – (Rev. 12:7-12). This results from the war in heaven at the midpoint of the Tribulation Period.
5. The Fifth Abode: The Abyss (aka. the Bottomless Pit) – (Rev. 20:1-3). This happens at the beginning of the Millennium.
6. The Sixth Abode: The Earth Revisited – (Rev. 20:3). This happens at the end of the Millennium and only lasts until the final Gog of Magog battle ends in Rev. 20:7-9.
7. The Seventh Abode: The Lake of Fire – (Rev. 20:10). Satan gets cast here after losing the battle in #6 above. According to the Bible, this is his final abode.

The Lake of Fire: Satan's Seventh and Final Abode

"The devil, who deceived them, was cast into the lake of fire and brimstone where the beast and the

false prophet *are*. And they will be tormented day and night forever and ever."
(Rev. 20:10)

The War in Heaven Happens at the Midpoint of the Tribulation

The biblical support for this prophecy finding fulfillment at the midpoint of the Tribulation Period is found in the fact that the event is sandwiched in between two key timing verses.

"Then the woman, (*Representing a believing remnant within Israel*), fled into the wilderness, (*In order to avoid persecution outsourced from Satan*), where she has a place prepared by God, that they should feed her there one thousand two hundred and sixty days."
(Rev. 12:6, NKJV; emphasis added)

"Now when the dragon saw that he had been cast to the earth, (*At the midpoint of the Tribulation Period*), he persecuted the woman, (*Israel*), who gave birth to the male *Child, (Jesus Christ)*. But the woman was given two wings of a great eagle, that she might fly into the wilderness to her place, where she is nourished for a time and times and half a time, (*Time = 1 year + Times = 2 years and half a time = ½ year totals 3 ½ years*), from the presence of the serpent."
(Rev. 12:13-14, NKJV; emphasis added)

The fleeing of the woman above, who represents the faithful Jewish remnant, into the wilderness happens during the second 3 ½ years of the Tribulation Period. After losing the war in heaven at the midpoint of the Tribulation Period, Satan immediately begins his persecution of the woman identified in these above verses.

The timeline below sequences the events in the middle of the Tribulation Period in the order that I believe they could happen. As the timeline depicts, in the aftermath of the war in heaven a flurry of powerful prophetic events happen in rapid succession.

1. Satan loses the war in heaven and he and the fallen angels are cast down to earth, (Rev. 12:7-12).
2. The Ten Kings desolate the Harlot World Religion, (Rev. 17:16).
3. The Antichrist dies and gets resurrected, (Rev. 13:3).
4. The Two Witnesses get killed, resurrect and then ascend to heaven, (Rev. 11:7-13).
5. The Abomination of Desolation gets set up in the Third Jewish Temple, (Daniel 9:27, Matthew 24:15).
6. The False Covenant gets annulled, (Isaiah 28:18, Daniel 9:27).
7. The Antichrist declares and shows himself as god, in the temple, (2 Thess. 2:4).
8. The Antichrist begins his genocidal campaign against the Jews, (Zechariah 13:8).
9. The False Prophet emerges, (Rev. 13:11-15).
10. The Mark of the Beast gets implemented, (Rev. 13:16-17).

Why the War in Heaven is a Woe Judgment

> "...Woe to the inhabitants of the earth and the sea! For the devil has come down to you, having great wrath, because he knows that he has a short time."
> (Rev. 12:12b)

The prior chapter identified the three Woe Judgments of the fifth, sixth and seventh trumpets, but the war in heaven ushers in another woe to the world. It's woeful for mankind because Satan and his fallen angelic cohorts are stuck on earth and they realize they only have a short time left, which according to prophecy is three and one-half years, until the Second Coming of Christ.

This critical timing means that these angelic rebels will likely be joining up with the untold number of demonic locusts from the Fifth Trumpet Judgment and the two hundred million demonic troops of the Sixth Trumpet Judgment. The last chapter pointed out that these fifth and sixth trumpet judgments happen before the midpoint of the Tribulation Period.

Moreover, we can presume that the locusts and the two hundred million demonic beings are still present on the earth at this time because demons don't die and they are not likely returning to the places of confinement from whence they escaped, which was the abyss for the locusts and the Euphrates for the two hundred million.

Similarly, angels don't die, so these rebellious defeated angels from the war in heaven are all coming down to inhabit the earth. We don't know the total headcount of all these bad angels, but according to Hebrews 12:22 there are myriads of angels. Some translations say they are an innumerable company.

"But you have come to Mount Zion and
to the city of the living God, the heavenly
Jerusalem, and to myriads of angels."
(Hebrews 22:12, NASB)

"But ye are come unto mount Sion, and unto the city
of the living God, the heavenly Jerusalem, and to an
innumerable company of angels."
(Hebrews 22:12, KJV)

It's possible that these evil angels are the same one-third spoken about in Revelation 12:4a, which says "*His*, (Satan's), *tail drew a third of the stars of heaven and threw them to the earth.*" In this usage "*the stars*" are a biblical typology for angels. We can surmise that these are rebellious angels because they are drawn to Satan. Good angels would oppose Satan and not be drawn to him. However, fallen angels would be drawn to Satan as his followers.

If there are about eight billion people on earth, then maybe there are at least that many angels in heaven, which is a significantly larger domain. Whatever the numerical equivalent of one third of the angels, it is likely in the thousands, if not the millions and possibly billions. It might even be possible that the demons enjoined with the fallen angels at this future point in time might equal or surpass the humans on earth, especially after the two hundred million demonic troops kill one-third of mankind prior as per Rev. 9:15,18.

Imagine the scenario for people on earth when this happens. Dear reader, you won't want to be living during this perilous period, nor do you want your loved ones to experience this sad state of affairs. Therefore, if you are reading this chapter during the Church Age, you and your loved ones still have time to escape these things by receiving Jesus Christ as your Lord and Savior. The Rapture of the Church will provide your foolproof earthly exit strategy!

Satan Loses the War and the Divine Debate

Revelation 12:10b says that Satan, *"is the accuser of our brethren, who accused them before our God day and night, has been cast down."*

Revelation 12:9 acknowledges that the Devil deceives the whole world, but the brethren in Rev. 12:10 are not falling for his lies. These brethren realize that as per John 14:6, "Jesus is the way, the truth, and the life." Rev. 12:11 says they overcome the great dragon's deceit *"by the blood of the Lamb and by the word of their testimony, and they did not love their lives to the death."*

These details narrow the identity of the "brethren" down to believers. Unbelievers are not covered by the blood of the Lamb, which was shed by Christ at the time of His crucifixion. More specifically, we can zoom closer in on this subset group of believers by understanding that historically, when Satan accuses someone before God, he is addressing a specific individual, someone relevant to the time of the accusation. Some of the examples of this are found in Job 1:6-12, 2:1-6 and Zechariah 3:1-5.

We can also eliminate the believers from the Church Age since those Christians have already been caught up to heaven in the Rapture and, as such it would serve no purpose for Satan to accuse them. The Apostle John states, "*the accuser of our brethren,*" inferring "*our*" is the Church and the "*brethren*" are the believers who get saved after the Church Age ends.

Thus, the brethren of Rev. 12:10 are people who get saved after the Rapture. These overcomers serve as God's rebuttal to Satan's campaign of deception. Satan had likely claimed during the Church Age that if he were fully freed from any restraint, he could dupe all of humanity through powerful signs and lying wonders into believing what 2 Thess. 2:11 calls, "The Lie." The Lie is a designed delusion that overtakes people who deny the truth.

These overcomers serve as a monkey wrench in the Devil's campaign and they provoke him to become an "accuser of our brethren." These accusations persist "before our God day and night." Thus, these brethren are Post-Rapture believers who receive Christ after the restraint upon Satan gets removed.

However, these Post-Rapture believers do not include those who get saved in the final 3 ½ years of the Tribulation Period because they come to faith after Satan has already been cast out of heaven at the midpoint of the Tribulation. Satan won't be able to accuse the believers of the second 3 ½ years of the tribulation before God in heaven because the Devil is gravity bound on earth.

So, it appears that the brethren being accused are those who get saved after the Rapture, but before the second 3 ½ years of the Tribulation Period. They, receiving Christ amidst Satan's unrestrained deception on earth, conclude the divine debate in heaven. These brethren saw through all the supernatural satanic deception and chose to receive Jesus Christ as their Savior even at the cost of severe persecution and possible martyrdom. Thus, the LORD can rest His case as Satan's accusations are all proven baseless.

With the conclusion of the divine debate, Satan's attempts to overstep God fail.

> "For you *(Satan)* have said in your heart: '**I will** ascend into heaven, **I will** exalt my throne above the stars of God; **I will** also sit on the mount of the congregation On the farthest sides of the north; **I will** ascend above the heights of the clouds, **I will** be like the Most High.'"
> (Isaiah 14:13-14; emphasis added)

Isaiah points out in the next verse that **NONE** of the five **I wills** above will happen. Satan will not ascend above the heights of the clouds like the Most High, but he will be sent to the lowest depths of the Bottomless Pit, which is his fifth abode.

> "Yet you shall be brought down to Sheol, To the lowest depths of the Pit." (Isaiah 14:15)

Having lost the divine debate, there is no longer a point for Satan to be lurking around in heaven and so he needs to leave. Apparently, the Devil doesn't want to depart voluntarily, but wages a war against Michael the Archangel in a final coup to overthrow God and maintain his residence in his third abode of the atmospheric heavens. Just like Satan loses the Divine Debate in Heaven he also loses the War in Heaven.

Conclusion

The war in heaven begins the rapid downfall of the Devil. He gets temporarily confined in his fourth abode, the earth, and then only 3 ½ years later at the end of the Tribulation Period he gets chained up in his fifth abode, the Bottomless Pit.

> "Then I saw an angel coming down from heaven,

having the key to the bottomless pit and a great chain in his hand. He laid hold of the dragon, that serpent of old, who is *the* Devil and Satan, and bound him for a thousand years; and he cast him into the bottomless pit, and shut him up, and set a seal on him, so that he should deceive the nations no more till the thousand years were finished. But after these things he must be released for a little while." (Rev. 20:1-3)

When Satan gets cast out of heaven in Rev. 12:9, he's not alone, but is accompanied by his rebellious angelic comrades. However, he soon loses his strength and the support of his follower angels. The above passage points out that a single no-name angel single-handedly, apparently without much of a fight, lays hold of the Devil and binds him up with a great chain for one thousand years.

The sequence of events that lead to Satan's rapid decline are as follows:

1. The restraint upon the Devil gets removed, (2 Thessalonians 2:7).

2. Satan employs supernatural deception to deceive mankind into believing "The Lie," (2 Thess. 2:9-12).

3. The Brethren, those who get saved after the Rapture, but before the second 3 ½ years of the Tribulation Period, don't fall for "The Lie," (Rev. 12:10).

4. Satan has them martyred, (Rev. 6:9-11), through the Harlot World Religion, (Rev. 17:6).

5. Satan is forced to find fault with these brethren in order to justify their martyrdoms.

6. Satan presents his accusations of these murdered Brethren before God and all the angels, good and bad, in the heavenly court, (Rev. 12:10).

7. The Devil's defense for causing their deaths does not win over God and Satan's accusations are thereby overruled.

8. Satan wages war against Michael and the good angels to avoid getting permanently evicted from heaven, (Rev. 12:7-8).

9. Michael wins and Satan and his fallen angels get cast down to earth and the doors to heaven are permanently locked to them, preventing their return, (Rev. 12:9).

10. Satan creates woeful conditions for the inhabitants of the earth during the last 3 ½ years of the Tribulation Period, (Rev. 12:12).

11. Jesus Christ returns in His Second Coming along with His good angels, (Matthew 16:27).

12. One of these good angels, apparently an ordinary angel, binds Satan with a great chain and casts that Devil into the Bottomless Pit for one thousand years, (Rev. 20:1-3).

13. Then, Isaiah 24:21, which was quoted at the start of this chapter and again below, finds final fulfillment.

"So it will happen on that day, That the Lord will punish the rebellious angels of heaven on high, And the kings of the earth on earth."
(Isaiah 24:21, NASB)

17

The Armageddon Campaign

The next two chapters will cover the series of phases that conclude with the epic battle identified in Revelation 16:14 as, "*the battle of that great day of God Almighty.*" This war takes place on a couple of battlefields, which will be acknowledged as the sequence of events are laid out.

Some call this the "Battle of Armageddon," but Armageddon is primarily a location for massive enemy troop assembling, rather than actual fighting. In fact, some suggest that no fighting even takes place there. Dr. Arnold Fruchtenbaum explains it this way.

> "*While the term "Battle of Armageddon" has been commonly used, it is really a misnomer, for more than one battle will take place. For this reason, many prophetic teachers ... are using the term "Campaign of Armageddon." But this, too, is a misnomer because there will be no fighting in Armageddon itself; all of the fighting will take place elsewhere.*"[51]

The Eleven Phases of the Armageddon Campaign

There appear to be eleven phases that comprise the Armageddon Campaign. They are listed in sequential order below. Then subsequently, each episode will be explained. Due to the quantity of information to be presented, only the first six phases will be covered in this chapter. The last five phases will be presented in the next chapter, which is entitled, "The Second Coming of Christ and the Armageddon Campaign."

> CAVEAT: these following phases and their chronological orders involve some speculation. They are scripturally supported, but admittedly some author liberties were taken.

1. The Fall of Jerusalem and Fleeing of the Faithful Jewish Remnant. Daniel 9:26-27
2. The Antichrist Invades and Desolates Egypt then Returns to Israel.
3. The LORD Strikes the Antichrist's Throne and Shuts Down his Global System, (The Fifth Bowl Judgment).
4. The Assembling of the Antichrist's Allied Armies at Armageddon. (These allied armies will be labeled as the "*Armageddonites*" within this chapter).
5. The Deployment of some of the Armageddonites to Bozrah.
6. The National Regeneration of Israel.

Phase 1: The Fall of Jerusalem and Fleeing of the Faithful Jewish Remnant

The Armageddon Campaign commences at the midpoint of the Seven Year Tribulation Period with the genocidal crusade of the Jews by the Antichrist. Why the Antichrist embarks upon this killing spree is explained later in this chapter. This complex conflict that will culminate in the Armageddonites assembling at Armageddon spans the entire second three and one-half years of the Tribulation Period.

The actual battling seemingly starts:

1. In Jerusalem,
2. Spreads throughout all of Israel, which should be a larger nation by then, than it is today,
3. Intensifies in ancient Edom, which is presently modern-day southern Jordan, but becomes part of Israel in the future.

4. Spills over into the Valley of Jehoshaphat, which is a valley near Jerusalem.

According to the prophet Joel, the Antichrist assembles some of his armies in the Valley of Jehoshaphat, which some suggest is the modern-day Kidron Valley to the east of Jerusalem.

> ""Proclaim this among the nations: "Prepare for war! Wake up the mighty men, Let all the men of war draw near, Let them come up. Beat your plowshares into swords And your hooks into spears; Let the weak say, 'I *am* strong.' " Assemble and come, all you nations, And gather together all around. Cause Your mighty ones to go down there, O Lord. "Let the nations be wakened, and come up to the Valley of Jehoshaphat; For there I will sit to judge all the surrounding nations.""
> (Joel 3:9-12)

Once assembled, these troops march into Jerusalem and rape, pillage and plunder the Jews and their neighborhoods.

> "Behold, the day of the Lord is coming, And your spoil will be divided in your midst. For I will gather all the nations to battle against Jerusalem; The city shall be taken, The houses rifled, And the women ravished. Half of the city shall go into captivity, But the remnant of the people shall not be cut off from the city."
> (Zechariah 14:1-2)

Jesus Christ warned the Jews in the prophetic verse below to flee immediately when the Antichrist started to make his move into the Jewish Temple, which will be built by then. He foreknew that after the Antichrist desecrated the Temple that he would command his troops to capture Jerusalem in fulfillment of Zechariah 14:2.

> "Therefore when you see the 'abomination of desolation,' spoken of by Daniel the prophet, standing in the holy place" (whoever reads, let him understand), "then let

> those who are in Judea flee to the mountains."
> (Matthew 24:15-16)

Jerusalem is where the Temple will be constructed and it is a central city in the territory of Judea. Jesus wasn't making a suggestion, rather He commanded "*whoever reads, let him understand.*" Understand what? Understand that a genocidal campaign is promptly forthcoming and two-thirds of the Jews living in Israel will be killed.

> " And it shall come to pass in all the land," Says the Lord, "*That* two-thirds in it shall be cut off *and* die, But *one*-third shall be left in it."
> (Zech. 13:8)

The one-third who survive represents those who understood that they needed to flee "*to the mountains*" as Christ instructed. They ultimately will represent national Israel because they are all the Jewish population that will survive. They are also alluded to as the Faithful Jewish Remnant.

> "I will bring the *one*-third through the fire, Will refine them as silver is refined, And test them as gold is tested. They will call on My name, And I will answer them. I will say, 'This *is* My people'; And each one will say, 'The Lord *is* my God.' "
> (Zech. 13:9)

It's important to consider that the Antichrist likely has to use force to enter into the Jewish Temple. This can be deduced by realizing that his multiple goals are to:

- Desecrate the Temple – (Daniel 9:27),
- Stop the sacrifices and offerings taking place therein – (Daniel 9:27),
- Set up his abomination, which some believe is the image of the Beast, (an image of himself) – (Revelation 13:14-15),
- Declare and show himself as god – (2 Thessalonians 2:4).

Certainly, Israel will attempt to prevent all of the above. However, they won't be able to stop him, which implies that he has assembled a significant amount of soldiers and weaponry to facilitate the fulfillment of his Temple invasion and Jerusalem killing plans.

Thus, Jerusalem falls and the wise Jews heed Christ's warnings and flee to the mountains. However, the foolish Jews stay behind. Perhaps, some of them flee from Jerusalem into other parts of Israel, but if they elect to remain inside of the country they will be hunted down as the battle spreads from Jerusalem into the rest of the nation.

Remember, Zechariah 13:8 informs that "*it shall come to pass in all the land,* (of Israel), *two-thirds in it shall...die.*" The slaughter is not confined to Jerusalem, but expands into Judah and throughout "*all the land.*" Isaiah provides details in the passage below about what Jewish life in "*all the land*" at that time will look like for those who decide to stick around.

"Your covenant with death will be annulled, And your agreement with Sheol will not stand; When the overflowing scourge passes through, Then you will be trampled down by it. As often as it goes out it will take you; For morning by morning it will pass over, And by day and by night; It will be a terror just to understand the report." For the bed is too short to stretch out *on,* And the covering so narrow that one cannot wrap himself *in it.*"

The covenant is the same one in Daniel 9:27 and Isaiah 28:15. It is the covenant that Israel will have signed onto three and one-half years earlier so that they could build their Third Temple and perform sacrifices and offerings therein. The overflowing scourge that passes through at this point represents the attempted genocide of the Jews by the Antichrist and his armies.

"*Morning by morning,*" "*by day and by night,*' Jews in Israel are captured and likely lined up in front of firing squads and killed. "*It will be a terror to understand the report*" of what's happening to the Jews on a daily basis inside of Israel. There won't likely be any concentration camps, whereby Jews are confined and deceived about their future fates like what happened in the Nazi Holocaust. No, the true intentions of these future Holocaust butchers will be perfectly understood by their victims.

Isaiah says, "*the bed is too short to stretch out on, And the covering so narrow that one cannot wrap himself in it.*" In other words, there will be no place inside "*all the land*" of Israel to hide out. There will be no hiding under beds or in blankets.

In summary of this section, over the course of three and one-half years of the second half of the Tribulation Period, "*two-thirds* (of the Jews in Israel) *in it shall be cut off and die.*" If you don't want any of your unsaved Jewish friends to go through this horrendous experience, then preach the Good News Gospel of Jesus Christ to them now!

Phase 2: The Antichrist Invades and Desolates Egypt then Returns to Israel

At some point during his Jew-killing campaign, the Antichrist invades Egypt.

> "He, (the Antichrist), will also invade the beautiful land, (of Israel), and many will fall. But these will escape from his power: Edom, Moab, and the prominent people[s] of the Ammonites. He will extend his power against the countries, and not even the land of Egypt will escape. He will get control over the hidden treasures of gold and silver and over all the riches of Egypt. The Libyans and Cushites, (Ethiopians), will also be in submission."
> (Daniel 11:41-43, HCSB; emphasis added)

While some of his troops are successfully executing Jews in all the *"beautiful land"* of Israel. The Antichrist marches with soldiers into Egypt. At that time, it appears that there will be Jews living in at least five cities of Egypt.

> "In that day there shall be five cities in the land of Egypt that speak the language of Canaan, (*Hebrew*), and swear to Jehovah of hosts; one shall be called The city of destruction."
> (Isaiah 19:18, ASV; emphasis added)

The elimination of these Hebrew-speaking Jews residing in these five cities will likely be a major reason why the Antichrist invades Egypt. Remember that the two-thirds of the Jews in *all the land*, which Daniel 11:41 identifies as *"the beautiful land,"* are destined to be killed. Some Bible translations call it *"the glorious land."* At this future point in time, the glorious land should include:

1. Five cities in Egypt – (Isaiah 19:18),
2. Jordan – (Jeremiah 49:2, Zephaniah 2:9 and Obadiah 1:19),
3. The West Bank, Golan Heights and Gaza Strip – (Obadiah 1:19),
4. Southern Lebanon (Zarephath) and perhaps the Sinai – (Obadiah 1:20).

For some reason, the Antichrist skirts by Jordan, (Edom, Moab and Ammon) and attacks Egypt. During his invasion, he desolates Egypt, which causes Egyptians to flee from the country. The prophet Ezekiel informs that Egypt will be desolate for forty years and the Egyptians will be dispersed out of the country throughout those forty years.

> "I will make the land of Egypt desolate in the midst of the countries that are desolate; and among the cities that are laid waste, her cities shall be desolate forty years; and I will scatter the Egyptians among

the nations and disperse them throughout the
countries." 'Yet, thus says the Lord God: "At the
end of forty years I will gather the Egyptians from
the peoples among whom they were scattered."
(Ezekiel 29:12-13)

The important question is, "did this forty years of desolation in Egypt ever happen historically?" If not, then this four-decade period is yet future. Incredibly, to my knowledge no historian has ever provided specific historical proof that these events did occur in the history of Egypt.

The fact that this prophecy remains unfulfilled means that the forty-year period begins at the latter part of the Tribulation Period, which implies that it overlaps into the Millennium. The verse below acknowledges that a time is forthcoming when Egypt will be a desolation.

"Egypt shall be a desolation, And Edom a desolate
wilderness, Because of violence *against* the people of
Judah, For they have shed innocent blood in their land."
(Joel 3:19)

Edom will be a desolate wilderness throughout the entire Millennium according to Isaiah 34:5-10, but Egypt's desolation will be temporary. Dr. Fruchtenbaum explains it this way.

"*With Edom, it will be total and permanent (desolation
and wilderness). But with Egypt, total yet temporary
(desolation but not a wilderness). In fact, the desolation of
Egypt is to last only for the first forty years of the Kingdom as
recorded in Ezekiel 29:1-16.*"[52]

After desolating Egypt, the Antichrist receives troubling news, which prompts him to return back into Israel. The upsetting information appears to be coming from southern Jordan, which would be to the northeast of his location in Egypt. The news report is likely that a sizeable remnant of Jews are hiding in the highly protective mountains of southern Jordan. These are the mountains

Then, all of a sudden in one hour, NOTHING! It will be lights out on the global system.

> "For in one hour such great riches came to nothing.' Every shipmaster, all who travel by ship, sailors, and as many as trade on the sea, stood at a distance and cried out when they saw the smoke of her burning, saying, 'What is like this great city?' "They threw dust on their heads and cried out, weeping and wailing, and saying, 'Alas, alas, that great city, in which all who had ships on the sea became rich by her wealth! For in one hour she is made desolate.'"
> (Rev. 18:17-19)

The passage above refers to the "great city" of the Antichrist's headquarters. Scholars are split as to what actual city this is because Revelation 17:5 describes it as a mystery. Some suggestions are a rebuilt Babylon in Iraq, New York City, Jerusalem, Mecca, or Rome.

In my book entitled, *The FINAL Prophecies, the Prophecies in the Last 3 ½ Years of the Tribulation*, I provide the reasons which strongly support that the great city is Rome. In that book, I also explain the likely length of time and extent of the darkness of the Fifth Bowl Judgment.

Whichever city it is, it's destroyed forever.

> "Then a mighty angel took up a stone like a great millstone and threw it into the sea, saying, "Thus with violence the great city Babylon shall be thrown down, and shall not be found anymore."
> (Rev. 18:21)

To counter the devastation, Rev. 16:14 informs that as part of the Sixth Bowl Judgment three powerful demonic spirits will perform miraculous signs *"to the kings of the earth and of the whole world, to gather them to the battle of that great day of God Almighty."*

Phase 4: The Assembling of the Antichrist's Allied Armies at Armageddon

> "And they gathered them together to the place called in Hebrew, Armageddon." (Rev. 16:14)

This verse tells us where the Armageddonites and their kings assemble for *"the battle of that great day of God Almighty."*

The ASV translation says, "And they gathered them together into the place which is called in Hebrew Har-Magedon."

Below is a comment about this ASV translation from Dr. Arnold Fruchtenbaum.

> *"Har-Magedon, as the ASV text shows,... is a combination of two Hebrew words which mean, 'the Mountain of Megiddo.' Megiddo was a strategic city located at the western end of the Valley of Jezreel, guarding the famous Megiddo Pass into Israel's largest valley. One can see the entire Valley of Jezreel from the mount upon which the city of Megiddo stood. So what is known as the Valley of Armageddon in Christian circles is actually the biblical Valley of Jezreel. The term Armageddon is never applied to the valley itself, but only to the mount at the western end. Here, in this large valley of Lower Galilee, the armies of the world will gather for the purposes of destroying all the Jews still living."*[53]

Firstly, observe that Dr. Fruchtenbaum concludes his comment by stating that, *"the armies of the world will gather for the purposes of destroying all the Jews still living."* This is the apparent war strategy of the Antichrist and his Armageddonites, and it will be discussed in greater detail in the next section of this chapter.

Fruchtenbaum further points out that Jezreel is the location of Israel's largest valley. The Valley of Jezreel is approximately 380 square kilometers, which is about 147 square miles. To put this in perspective, it is slightly larger than the entire city of Philadelphia, which is Pennsylvania's largest city. Philadelphia measures about 142 square miles.

This valley is not only spacious but it's lush and fertile according to the Wikipedia quote below.

"The Jezreel Valley is a green fertile plain covered with fields of wheat, watermelon, melon, oranges, white beans, cowpeas, chickpeas, green beans, cotton sunflowers and corn, as well as grazing tracts for multitudes of sheep and cattle."[54]

Thus, the territorial size, level terrain and agricultural supply makes it the choice destination for the deployment of the multitude of Armageddonite troops.

The French military and political leader Napoleon Bonaparte, who is widely considered one of the greatest military generals in history, once stood at the valley of Megiddo and stated, *"All the armies of the world could maneuver their forces on this vast plain."* In 1799 Napoleon fought near this valley and declared that it's *"the most natural battleground of the whole Earth."*

Another attribute of the Valley of Jezreel is that hosts the site of the Megiddo Airfield, known as Shachar 7 by the Israel Defense Forces. It is an Israeli airfield located in the Jezreel Valley near Tel Megiddo and is used as an auxiliary field for the Ramat David Israeli Air Force Base. This important runway, if it's still intact at the time, will facilitate the transporting of troops, weapons and supplies for the epic battle.

The Valley of Jezreel vs. The Valley of Hamon Gog

On a side note, in addition to the Valley of Jezreel, the Valley of Hamon Gog will be a different, but notable valley in the end times. The Valley of Hamon Gog doesn't exist yet, but it will become the location of the burial grounds of the corpses of the Magog invaders of Ezekiel 38 and 39. This was mentioned in an earlier chapter of this book entitled, "Ezekiel 38-39, When God Upholds His Holy Name."

> "It will come to pass in that day that I will give Gog a burial place there in Israel, the valley of those who pass by east of the sea; and it will obstruct travelers, because there they will bury Gog and all his multitude. Therefore they will call it the Valley of Hamon Gog. For seven months the house of Israel will be burying them, in order to cleanse the land."
> (Ezekiel 39:11-12)

I suspect that the valley located "east of the sea" refers to the territory in Central Jordan, which is east of the Dead Sea. If my location speculation is correct, then the Armageddonites will likely have to march southwestward through this valley enroute to reach their Jewish targets, who will be hiding out in refuge within the steep mountains of southern Jordan in Petra. Southern Jordan is where a majority of the fighting seems to take place. This statement will be qualified later in this chapter.

Wherever the valley "east of the sea" is located, its existence in the Mideast will serve as a reminder to the Armageddonites of the supernatural defeat of the Magog invaders by the Lord. This miraculous victory is described in Ezekiel 38:18-39:6. The God that stopped the Magog invaders dead in their tracks is the same God that the Armageddonites intend to defeat, discredit and abolish.

The War Strategy of the Antichrist and the Armageddonites

The apparent war strategy to defeat the LORD is to annihilate the Chosen Jewish People and permanently possess the Promised Land of Israel. The LORD has guaranteed that there is only one way that this feat can be accomplished, and that method is summed up below.

> "Thus says the LORD, Who gives the sun for a light by day, The ordinances of the moon and the stars for a light by night, Who disturbs the sea, And its waves roar (The LORD of hosts is His name): "If those ordinances depart From before Me, says the LORD, Then the seed of Israel (the Promised Land) shall also cease From being a nation before Me forever." Thus says the LORD: "If heaven above can be measured, And the foundations of the earth searched out beneath, I will also cast off all the seed of Israel (the Chosen People) For all that they have done, says the LORD.""
> (Jeremiah 31:35-37; emphasis added)

The problem for the Antichrist and his Armageddonites is that they are incapable of accomplishing the above requirements. As such, they go to plan B, which is to annihilate the Chosen People. If there are no more Jews then there is no more need for Israel as the Promised Land.

Moreover, if there are no more Jews, then Jesus Christ will not be able to fulfill the promised prophecy of His Second Coming, which is spelled out below.

> "for I, (*Jesus Christ*), say to you, (*the Jews of national Israel*). you shall see Me no more till you say, 'Blessed is He who comes in the name of the Lord!' "
> (Matthew 23:39; emphasis added)

The Jewish religious leaders had rejected Jesus Christ as the Messiah at His First Coming, so Jesus mandated that He would not return in His Second Coming until future Jewish leaders say, '*Blessed is He who comes in the name of the Lord!*'

Bible prophecy expert John MacArthur speculates this below as a possible Armageddonite strategy for this final battle.

> "*It is also possible… that their last-ditch effort to stop all of this,* (God's judgments), *somehow involves the destruction of any remaining Jews in the land of Israel. Maybe this is a final act of rabid antisemitism to destroy the remaining Jews. Now you remember the Lord is going to hide some Jews. And we learn about that back in* (Revelation) *chapter 12. They're going to be protected and nourished for that second half of the Tribulation time, and maybe they're* (the Armageddonites) *going to come and rout them out and massacre them all in hopes that God will tuck His tail and go away and hide and leave them alone.*"
> (Author emphasis added)

If MacArthur's assessment is correct, then what a foolish strategy on behalf of the Antichrist. The plan is to massacre the faithful Jewish remnant "*in hopes that God will tuck His tail and go away and hide and leave them alone.*" What are the Armageddonites planning? Are they audaciously thinking that when Jesus Christ comes to rescue the remnant in hiding, that they can ambush Him and cut Him off at the pass?

Thus, the motivation of the Antichrist is to kill all the Jews so that he can prevent the return of Jesus Christ in the Second Coming. If there are no Jews alive, then there will be none left to say, "*Blessed is He Who comes in the name of the Lord.*"

Moreover, by eliminating the Jewish race, the Antichrist also discredits the covenant-keeping character of the LORD, Who had promised Abraham that he would have descendants and a homeland forever. These descendants are the Jews.

> "For all the land which you see I give to you and your descendants forever. And I will make your descendants as the dust of the earth; so that if a man could number the dust of the earth, then your descendants also could be numbered."
> (Genesis 13:15-16)

The Seventh Bowl Judgment

While the Armageddonites deploy to Armageddon, the LORD levies His second major attack upon them, which is described in the Seventh Bowl Judgment.

> "Now the great city was divided into three parts, and the cities of the nations fell. And great Babylon was remembered before God, to give her the cup of the wine of the fierceness of His wrath. Then every island fled away, and the mountains were not found. And great hail from heaven fell upon men, *each hailstone* about the weight of a talent. Men blasphemed God because of the plague of the hail, since that plague was exceedingly great."
> (Revelation 16:19-21)

As the kings of the earth muster up their courage and make their march to the valley of Armageddon for *the battle of that great day of God Almighty*, they become slow-moving targets, or essentially, sitting ducks, for the Lord's one-two punch combo. The earth shakes mightily beneath their feet as God extends *His left jab* and then canon ball size hailstones pummel them from above as God delivers *His right cross* punch! Each hailstone will weigh the equivalent of a Hebrew talent measurement which is estimated to be about 57 pounds.[55]

Some prophecy teachers estimate the weight of each hailstone to be even heavier than 57 pounds.

> "*The hail reminds us of the seventh plague (Ex. 9:22-26). Imagine hailstones that weigh 125 pounds, which is what a talent of silver weighed in John's day.*" (Warren Wiersbe)[56]

> "*In addition to the earthquake, huge hailstones of about 100 pounds each fell on people. Such huge masses of ice supernaturally formed would destroy anything left standing from the earthquake and would no doubt kill or seriously injure those they hit.*" (John Walvoord)[57]

After dodging the barrage of heaven-sent bombs, these Armageddonites will likely wonder if the powerful earthquake they experienced was so mighty that many of their hometowns were reduced to rubble as they hear that, "*the cities of the nations fell.*"

As a result of the LORD's *one-two punch combo*, the Armageddonites have to go the distance and finish the fight against God. This is because many of them no longer have a place of retreat since some of their cities have been destroyed by the great earthquake. Adding to their stress is the daunting possibility, that if their hometowns were toppled, their family and friends were probably buried beneath the rubble, that is if they survived the hailstone assault!

Now might be a suitable time to ask you, especially if you are an unbeliever, what God asked His servant Job in ancient times.

"Have you entered, *or seen*, the treasury of snow, Or have you seen the treasury of hail, Which I have reserved for the time of trouble, For the day of battle and war?" (Job 38:22-23, NKJV; emphasis added)

The Armageddonites will be forced to answer this question with an emphatic; "*YES, WE HAVE SEEN THE LORD'S TREASURY, OR SHALL WE SAY, ARMORY OF HAIL!*"

How mighty could this unprecedented earthquake be? The quotes below might help to put the power of this super quake into perspective.

"*A 9.0 earthquake can cause: At or near total destruction – severe damage or collapse to all buildings. Heavy damage and shaking extends to distant locations. Permanent changes in ground topography.*"[58]

"*A magnitude 9.0 earthquake on Richter scale is equivalent to release of energy by 25,000 nuclear bombs. So a 10.0 magnitude earthquake will be analogous to dropping over 400,000 nuclear* bombs at a time. *This is enough to destroy anything and everything on earth if it is a point source on the surface.*"[59]

Whatever the scientific seismic equivalent is, the details of this earthquake are clear. Some "great city" gets split into three parts, cities within nations collapse, islands become detached from their foundations and mountains disappear. We are informed that when it's all said and done, the surviving Armageddonite soldiers and the still living civilians they left behind, *"blasphemed God because of the plague of the hail, since that plague was exceedingly great."*

Phase 5: *The Deployment of some of the Armageddonites to Bozrah*

In an attempt to kill the Jewish remnant that has fled to southern Jordan for safety, the Antichrist will deploy troops and necessary military equipment to Bozrah, which appears to be modern-day Basira. According to the passages below this is where Jesus Christ arrives in His Second Coming to fight the Armageddonites and subsequently rescue the Jewish remnant. Bozrah is located in ancient Edom (southern Jordan).

> "For My, (*Jesus Christ*), sword shall be bathed in heaven; Indeed it shall come down, (*at the Second Coming*), on Edom, And on the people, (*the Armageddonites*), of My curse, for judgment. The sword of the Lord is filled with, (*the Armageddonites*), blood, It is made overflowing with fatness, With the blood of lambs and goats, With the fat of the kidneys of rams. For the Lord has a sacrifice in Bozrah, And a great slaughter in the land of Edom."
> (Isaiah 34:5-6; emphasis added)

> "Who *is* this who comes from Edom, With dyed garments from Bozrah, This *One who is* glorious in His apparel, Traveling in the greatness of His strength?— "I, (*Jesus Christ*), who speak in righteousness, mighty to save." Why *is* Your apparel red, And Your garments like one who treads in the winepress? "I have trodden

the winepress alone, And from the peoples no one *was* with Me. For I have trodden them in My anger, And trampled them in My fury; Their, (*Armageddonites*), blood is sprinkled upon My garments, And I have stained all My robes. For the day of vengeance *is* in My heart, And the year of My redeemed, (*the Faithful Jewish Remnant*), has come. I looked, but *there was* no one to help, And I wondered That *there was* no one to uphold; Therefore My own arm brought salvation for Me; And My own fury, it sustained Me. I have trodden down the, (*Armageddonites*), peoples in My anger, Made them drunk in My fury, And brought down their strength to the earth.""
(Isaiah 63:1-6; emphasis added)

The Jewish remnant will be hiding in Petra, Jordan. Petra is located at the southern part of the mountains in southern Jordan. In ancient times these mountains were called Mount Seir.

"Mount Seir is the ancient and biblical name for a mountainous region stretching between the Dead Sea and the Gulf of Aqaba in the northwestern region of Edom and southeast of the Kingdom of Judah."[60]

Conversely, Basira (Bozrah) where the bloody fighting takes place by Jesus Christ against the Armageddonites, is located near the northern part of the Mount Seir mountain range. The likely reason the Armageddonites deploy there rather than advance directly to the town of Wadi Musa, which is adjacent to Petra, is because the main roads in Jordan that are capable of facilitating the massive troop and equipment movement seem to filter through Basira. These armed convoys will likely travel on Kings Highway that runs through the heart of Basira.

(You are encouraged at this point to open up Google Maps on the Internet and search for the Kings Highway 35 in Jordan. Then, follow it as it courses through Basira and skirts southward along the eastside of Jordan's southern mountain range and makes it way to Wadi Musa. This is the possible route the Armageddonites might chart out).

Basira appears to be the most suitable staging area for a final advance upon Petra. It's a city that appears to be spread out enough to handle a large number of troops and artillery. The Armageddonites will have to rely on these ground forces to make sure that every last Jew is eliminated.

Air strikes could be employed as part of the campaign, but due to the rugged mountain terrain where the Jewish remnant will be hiding, soldiers will need to make the final sweep through the area. They won't likely be instructed to take prisoners, but rather to ensure that there are no Jewish survivors.

Phase 6: The National Regeneration of Israel

When the Jewish remnant gets word that the Armageddonites are stationed in Basira and ready to attack Petra, they will recognize that Jesus Christ is the Messiah and realize that He is their only hope for survival.

This remnant represents national Israel, and they will cry out. "*Blessed is He who comes in the name of the Lord!*" Hosea prophesied about this remnant in the verse below.

> "I, (*Jesus Christ*), will return again to My place, (*ascend into heaven*), Till they, (*the Jewish remnant*) acknowledge their offense, (*national and generational rejection of Jesus as the Messiah*). Then they will seek My face; In their affliction, (*when the Armageddonites are coming to kill them*), they will earnestly seek Me."
> (Hosea 5:15; emphasis added)

Thus, the nation of Israel becomes a saved nation in fulfillment of the verse below.

> "And so all Israel will be saved, as it is written: "The Deliverer, (*Jesus the Messiah*), will come out of Zion,

And He will turn away ungodliness from Jacob, (*Israel*)."
(Romans 11:26; emphasis added)

Pinpointing Petra as the Place of Refuge for the Remnant

Isaiah 34 and 63 point out that Christ will fight the Armageddonites in Edom and more specifically in Bozrah, but how do we pinpoint Petra as the place of refuge for the Jewish remnant? Why aren't they hiding in Bozrah? This segment and the *Why Petra* section below will explain why.

> "God came from Teman, And the Holy One from mount Paran. *Selah* His glory covered the heavens, And the earth was full of his praise."
> (Habakkuk 3:3)

This verse applies to the Second Coming of Jesus Christ. It is sometimes used to support the whereabouts of the Jewish remnant. After they are rescued by Jesus Christ, He will lead them back to Israel from "Teman" and "mount Paran." Two locations are identified.

Teman was the name of an Edomite clan. It was also an ancient biblical town called Arabia Petraea, which was part of the Nabatean Kingdom. The capital city of Arabia Petraea was Petra.[61]

Mount Paran, appears to be located within the "wilderness of Paran." Below are a few quotes that seem to place the wilderness of Paran in Edom.

> "*Paran is a large wilderness area that extends from Petra (Kadesh Barnea) down to Midian, east of the Arabah valley.*"[62]

> "*The name Paran most often occurs in the Old Testament as 'Wilderness of Paran' (Gn 21:21; Nm 10:12; 12:16; 13:3, 26). The Wilderness of Paran was the area encompassed by the Wadi Paran and its tributaries, extending from approximately*

the midpoint of the Arabah Valley between the Dead Sea and the Gulf of Aqaba/Elat, southwest to the Trans-Sinai Highway. That the Trans-Sinai Highway went through the Wilderness of Paran is evident from 1 Kings 11:18. When Hadad, heir to the throne of Edom, was taken to Egypt for safety during David's reign, his retinue followed the same route Moses took centuries earlier. Starting from Midian, they traveled to Paran then on to Egypt."[63]

"*A city by the name of Teman existed not far from Petra. Habakkuk 3:3 shows the area of Teman in parallel with Mount Paran, which some consider to be a poetic reference to Mount Sinai, but it more likely refers to Mount Seir in central Edom. It is helpful to remember that some of the prophecies concerning Esau use Teman as an alternative name for Edom.*"[64]

Why Petra?

This might be a good time to answer the question of why the Jewish remnant is hiding in Petra, rather than Haifa, Tel Aviv, Jerusalem or other notable Israeli cities. They will have fled there for one or more of the reasons listed below.

1. *Avoiding genocide:* They are attempting to escape from the genocidal campaign of the Antichrist, (Zechariah 13:8-14:2).

2. *No safe cities inside of Israel:* Haifa, Tel Aviv, Jerusalem and every other city in Israel will be under siege and unsafe to hide out in. (Isaiah 28:19-20)

3. *Following the commands of Christ:* They are following the instructions of Jesus Christ that are inscribed in the passage below. Christ says, "*flee to the mountains,*" which according to Isaiah 34 and 63 are the mountains in Edom of southern Jordan. Petra is located within these mountains. We can determine this location because this is where Jesus Christ returns on behalf of the Jewish remnant according to Isaiah's passages.

> "Therefore when you see the 'abomination of desolation,' spoken of by Daniel the prophet, standing in the holy place" (whoever reads, let him understand), "then let those who are in Judea flee to the mountains (*in Edom*)."
> (Matthew 24:15-16; emphasis added)

4. *Seeking a safe haven*: Petra is located within these steep mountains in Southern Jordan. Their layout serves as an impenetrable rock fortress of protection. Moreover, there are many hand-hewn caves carved into the mountains that provide shelter. These caves were once home to the ancient Edomites and then later to the Nabateans. National Geographic has called it the "Lost City."

> "*Petra was once a thriving trading center and the capital of the Nabataean empire between 400 B.C. and A.D. 106.*"[65]

5. *Seeking a safe passage*: Jordan will likely belong to Israel at the time according to prophecies in Jeremiah 49:2, Zephaniah 2:8-9 and Ezekiel 25:12-14. These prophecies find fulfillment prior to the Tribulation Period and concern Ammon, Moab and Edom, which respectively represent northern, central and southern Jordan today. This is an important note, otherwise access to Petra of a million plus Jewish refugees would undoubtedly be prohibited by the current Jordanian government.

6. *Petra is a place prepared by God:* Revelation 12 tells us that this is a place in the wilderness that is prepared by God to protect the Jewish Remnant in the last three and one-half years of the Tribulation, which coincides with the timing of the Jewish genocidal campaign of the Antichrist.

> "Then the woman, (*Israel*), fled into the wilderness, where she has a place prepared by God, that they should feed her there one thousand two hundred and sixty days."
> (Rev. 12:6; emphasis added)

> "Now when the dragon, (*Satan*), saw that he had been cast to the earth, (*at the midpoint of the tribulation*), he persecuted the woman, (*Israel*), who gave birth to the male *Child, (Jesus Christ, Who is a Jew)*. But the woman was given two wings of a great eagle, that she might fly into the wilderness, (*Petra*), to her place, where she is nourished for a time, (*one year*), and times, (*two years*), and half a time (*half year*), from the presence of the serpent, (*Satan*). So the serpent spewed water out of his mouth like a flood after the woman, that he might cause her to be carried away by the flood. But the earth helped the woman, and the earth opened its mouth and swallowed up the flood which the dragon had spewed out of his mouth."
> (Rev. 12:13-16; emphasis added)

Jesus instructed the Jewish remnant in Matthew 24:15 to flee to the mountains, which are in the wilderness area of southern Jordan, because He knew the place would be prepared for them by God. It's interesting to note a few things about Petra.

1. It's almost impenetrable and is limited to three pathways of entrance. They are identified as the "Backdoor," "Classic Front" and "Side Entrance."[66]

2. There are multiple dwelling and assembly places that were elaborately sculpted by the Nabateans by 312 BC and before. Some of these cave dwellings have multiple carved-out sleeping quarters.

3. Petra is presently a designated archaeological park that is managed and protected by the Ministry of Tourism and Antiquities. This is keeping Petra preserved from Bedouin squatting and littering.

> "The Bedouins lived in the caves and caverns of Petra — which they called "al-Mughar" — until 1985, when the Jordanian government forced them to evacuate the city's caves and archaeological sites."[67]

4. Two lengthy water canals have been carved out of the rock by the Nabateans. One was used for drinking and potable purposes and the other for agricultural purposes. It will be highly likely that the LORD will fill these canals with an ample supply of water to help the Jewish remnant survive.

The Petra Water Channels

"Channels were carved into the mountainous terrain to divert and focus runoff water to the nearby dams and cisterns, improving the rainwater capture efficiency. Other channels were carved into the rock to accommodate and support the clay pipes that distributed the water."

The Petra Pipelines

"Evidence of over 200 kilometers (125 miles) of mostly clay pipelines have been discovered in and around Petra. The pipelines were designed and positioned to transport and distribute the water throughout the city of Petra. The Petra water system evolved over hundreds of years to become a complex system which connected reservoirs, cisterns, dams and basins to the inhabitants and structures of Petra."[68]

(Phases seven to eleven are presented in the next chapter).

18

The Second Coming of Christ and the Armageddon Campaign

This chapter is part two of the Armageddon Campaign. It presents phases seven to eleven of this last days campaign. The first six phases were covered in the prior chapter called, "*The Armageddon Campaign.*" These final five phases are listed in sequential order below. Then subsequently, each episode will be explained.

Phases Seven - Eleven of the Armageddon Campaign

7. The Second Coming of Jesus Christ.
8. The Battle at Bozrah between Christ and the Armageddonites.
9. The Assembling of the Armies of Christ from Heaven.
10. The Battle in the Valley of Jehoshaphat.
11. The Victory Ascent Up the Mount of Olives and Return of the Jewish Remnant.

Phase 7: The Second Coming of Jesus Christ

Phase 6 pointed out that the Savior, Jesus Christ, won't get stranded in heaven, but will return to the earth a second time when the Faithful Jewish Remnant gets regenerated. They utter the all-important words, "*Blessed is He who comes in the name of the Lord,*" and without delay Jesus Christ returns. It will be a grand entrance!

> "Then the sign of the Son of Man will appear in heaven, and then all the tribes of the earth will mourn, and they will see the Son of Man coming on the clouds of heaven with power and great glory."
> (Matthew 24:30)

> "Behold, He is coming with clouds, and every eye will see Him, even they who pierced Him. And all the tribes of the earth will mourn because of Him. Even so, Amen."
> (Rev. 1:7)

Phase 8: The Battle at Bozrah between Christ and the Armageddonites

His first stop on his return to earth appears to be Basira (Bozrah). The telling verses that point this out are found in Isaiah 34:5-6 and Isaiah 63:1-6. These verses were already quoted in the Phase 5 section of the previous chapter. A few of the noteworthy highlights from these passages are below.

1. The sword of the Lord is filled with blood, (Isaiah 34:6).
2. The Lord has a sacrifice in Bozrah, And a great slaughter in the land of Edom, (Isaiah 34:6).
3. This One Who travels in the greatness of His strength and speaks in righteousness and is mighty to save, (Isaiah 63:1).
4. His garments are stained with Armageddonite blood, (Isaiah 63:3).
5. He comes on the day of vengeance and the year of His redeemed, alluding to the rescuing of the Faithful Jewish Remnant, (Isaiah 63:4).
6. He comes alone and fights the Armageddonites single-handedly, (Isaiah 63:5).

Phase 9: *The Assembling of the Armies of Christ from Heaven*

The highlights just provided in Phase 8 are important because they help to understand what's taking place in Phase 9. With the defeat of many Armageddonite troops at Bozrah (Phase 8), We shift our focus to Revelation 19.

> "Now I saw heaven opened, and behold, a white horse. And He who sat on him *was* called Faithful and True, and in righteousness He judges and makes war. His eyes *were* like a flame of fire, and on His head *were* many crowns. He had a name written that no one knew except Himself. He *was* clothed with a robe dipped in blood, (*from the Bozrah battle*) and His name is called The Word of God, (*Jesus Christ*). And the armies in heaven, clothed in fine linen, white and clean, followed Him on white horses." (Rev. 19:11-14; emphasis added)

After His major victory in the ground battle fought at Bozrah, Christ appears to go airborne temporarily back up to heaven. His robe is already "*dipped in blood*" from the battle at Bozrah. His heavenly armies are wearing "*white and clean*" clothes because Christ fought single-handedly at Bozrah and they didn't participate in that blood bath. Otherwise, their clothes would likewise be stained with blood.

This scene appears to position Christ in heaven, rather than on earth because when He returns to earth for a second round of fighting, the armies in heaven "*followed Him on white horses.*"

The apostle John sees Christ on a white horse. We know this refers to Jesus because He's called "*The Word of God,*" which is in alignment with the verses below.

"In the beginning was the Word, and the Word was with God, and the Word was God." (John 1:1)

'And the Word became flesh and dwelt among us, and we beheld His glory, the glory as of the only begotten of the Father, full of grace and truth." (John 1:14)

John declares that *"He judges and makes war."* We already realize from phase 8 that Christ knows how to successfully make war, but now He has to make more war and subsequently execute judgments upon the civilian populations, both good and bad, that are still alive on earth.

These judgments are accomplished after all the fighting is finished, but before Christ reigns in the Millennium. The judgment process is described in the Sheep and Goat Gentile judgments of Matthew 25:31-46. I write about these judgments in my book entitled, *The MILLENNIUM Prophecies and the NEW JERUSALEM*.

The armies returning with Christ include the good angels. They will play a significant role in the Sheep and Goat judgments, in that they will be instrumental in gathering up the Gentiles for the judgments. They will also participate in the execution of the judgment of the unsaved Goat Gentiles.

"When the Son of Man comes in His glory, and all the holy angels with Him, then He will sit on the throne of His glory. All the nations will be gathered before Him, and He will separate them one from another, as a shepherd divides *his* sheep from the goats."
(Matt. 25:31-32)

"And to *give* you who are troubled rest with us when the Lord Jesus is revealed from heaven with His mighty angels, in flaming fire taking vengeance on those who do not know God, and on those who do not obey the gospel of our Lord Jesus Christ. These shall be punished with everlasting destruction from the presence of the Lord and from the glory of His power." (2 Thessalonians 1:7-9)

"So it will be at the end of the age. The angels will come forth, separate the wicked from among the just, and cast them into the furnace of fire. There will be wailing and gnashing of teeth." (Matt. 13:49-50)

These angels are also involved in gathering any surviving saved Jews living throughout the world.

"And He will send His angels with a great sound of a trumpet, and they will gather together His elect from the four winds, from one end of heaven to the other." (Matthew 24:31)

As per Revelation 19:19, these angels will also be involved in the remainder of the fighting, which will be pointed out next in phase 10.

Phase 10: The Battle in the Valley of Jehoshaphat

Round two of the fighting between Jesus Christ and the Armageddonites happens next.

"Now out of His mouth goes a sharp sword, that with it He should strike the nations. And He Himself will rule them with a rod of iron. He Himself treads the winepress of the fierceness and wrath of Almighty God."
(Rev. 19:15)

Jesus Christ returns on His white horse with the heavenly army and He brings a sharp sword along to strike the remaining Armageddonites.

"And I saw the beast (*Antichrist*), the kings of the earth, and their (*Armageddonite*) armies, gathered together to make war against Him, (*Jesus Christ*), who sat on the

(*White*) horse and against His (*heavenly*) army."
(Rev. 19:19; emphasis added)

Jesus Christ is heading into battle with His heavenly army to defeat the Antichrist and his international armies. According to Joel 3:9-12, quoted earlier, these Armageddonites are all psyched up, their weapons are locked and loaded, and stationed in the Valley of Jehoshaphat, which is the modern-day Kidron Valley.

Alluding to the location of the Antichrist, Daniel 11:45 points out that *"the tents of his palace is between the seas and the glorious holy mountain,"* and that this is where his tyrannic reign on earth will end. Joel 3:9-12 seemingly pinpoints his location in the vicinity between Jerusalem and the Kidron Valley.

The next two verses inform that Christ will overthrow the Antichrist and then cast him and the False Prophet alive into the Lake of Fire.

"And then the lawless, (*the Antichrist*), one will be revealed, whom the Lord Jesus will overthrow with the breath of his mouth and destroy by the splendor of his coming." (2 Thess. 2:8, NIV; emphasis added)

"Then the beast, (*the Antichrist*), was captured, and with him the false prophet who worked signs in his presence, by which he deceived those who received the mark of the beast and those who worshiped his image. These two were cast alive into the lake of fire burning with brimstone." (Rev. 19:20; emphasis added)

As a result of the fighting, the Armageddonites are all killed by the sharp sword that Christ wields.

"And the rest (*of the Armageddonites*) were killed with the sword which proceeded from the mouth of Him who sat on the horse. And all the birds were filled with their flesh." (Rev. 19:21; emphasis added)

The slain Armageddonite bodies become a sacrificial meal for the vultures nesting in Israel.

> "Then I saw an angel standing in the sun; and he cried with a loud voice, saying to all the birds that fly in the midst of heaven, "Come and gather together for the supper of the great God, that you may eat the flesh of kings, the flesh of captains, the flesh of mighty men, the flesh of horses and of those who sit on them, and the flesh of all *people,* free and slave, both small and great."
> (Rev. 19:17-18)

This will be the second feast for these birds of prey. The first feast was in the aftermath of the defeat of the Magog invaders in Ezekiel 39:17-20.

Some teach that the manner in which Christ strikes these enemy armies is described in the verse below.

> "And this shall be the plague with which the Lord will strike all the people who fought against Jerusalem: Their flesh shall dissolve while they stand on their feet, Their eyes shall dissolve in their sockets, And their tongues shall dissolve in their mouths." (Zechariah 14:12)

Whatever method of warfare Christ employs, the blood of these slain troops is spread out for about seventy-five miles.

> "And the winepress, (*bloody battlefield*), was trampled outside the city, (*of Jerusalem*), and blood came out of the winepress, up to the horses' bridles, for one thousand six hundred furlongs, (*75 miles*)."
> (Rev. 14:20; emphasis added)

Phase 11: The Victory Ascent Up the Mount of Olives and Return of the Jewish Remnant

Once the fighting is done and the Armageddonites are all dead and the Antichrist is kicked off the planet and cast into the Lake of Fire, it's safe for the Faithful Jewish Remnant to return home to Israel. Apparently, Jesus escorts them out of Petra and leads them through the former battle zone of Bozrah.

> "Someday, O Israel, I will gather you; I will gather the remnant who are left. I will bring you together again like sheep in a pen, (*Bozrah*), like a flock in its pasture. Yes, your land will again be filled with noisy crowds! Your leader will break out and lead you out of exile, out through the gates of the enemy cities, back to your own land. Your king will lead you; the Lord himself will guide you."
> (Micah 2:12-13, NIV; emphasis added)

The above passage uses the word pen, but it's the Hebrew word Bozrah. This passage and the differing translations of it below, help to chart the route of their return, the size of the remnant population and the elated mindsets they share.

> "I will surely assemble, O Jacob, all of thee; I will surely gather the remnant of Israel; I will put them together as the sheep of Bozrah, as a flock in the midst of their pasture; they shall make great noise by reason of *the multitude of men.*"
> (Micah 2:12, ASV)

> "One who breaks open the way will advance before them; they will break out, pass through the gate, and leave by it. Their King will pass through before them, the LORD as their leader."
> (Micah 2:13, HCSB)

Since Bozrah means sheepfold, it seems fitting that Jesus Christ, the good shepherd as per John 10:11-18, should lead them back to their homeland through the city whose name means sheepfold. However, more than the symbolism of the name, is the fact that the remnant can feel relieved that their Savior has returned and rid them of their Armageddonite enemies.

Passing through this bloody battlefield, they will witness firsthand, the fulfillment of the slaughter predicted in Isaiah 34:6; *"For the Lord has a sacrifice in Bozrah and a great slaughter in the land of Edom."*

Joel 3:19 points out that Edom will ultimately become a desolate wilderness because of the violence they committed and the innocent Jewish blood that they shed against the people of Judah and the land of Israel.

The Jeremiah and Isaiah passages below also point out that Edom will be filled with plagues and unfit for human habitation forever.

> "Edom also shall be an astonishment; Everyone who goes by it will be astonished And will hiss at all its plagues. As in the overthrow of Sodom and Gomorrah And their neighbors," says the Lord, "No one shall remain there, Nor shall a son of man dwell in it."
> (Jer. 49:17-18)

> "For *it is* the day of the Lord's vengeance, The year of recompense for the cause of Zion. Its, (*Edom's*) streams shall be turned into pitch, And its dust into brimstone; Its land shall become burning pitch. It shall not be quenched night or day; Its smoke shall ascend forever. From generation to generation it shall lie waste; No one shall pass through it forever and ever."
> (Isaiah 34:8-10; emphasis added)

In Micah 2:12, the remnant is identified as a *"multitude of men."* They apparently become a jubilant *"noisy crowd"* as they travel through and witness the devastation at Bozrah. Christ will lead them on to their next destination, which will appear to be the Mount of Olives. This is a mountain ridge east of and adjacent to Jerusalem's Old City.

> "And in that day His, (*Jesus Christ's*), feet will stand on the Mount of Olives, Which faces Jerusalem on the east. And the Mount of Olives shall be split in two, From east to west, *Making* a very large valley; Half of the mountain shall move toward the north And half of it toward the south." (Zechariah 14:4; emphasis added).

In the quote below, Dr. Arnold Fruchtenbaum calls this Christ's "Victory Ascent."

> "*After the actual fighting is completed, there will be a victory ascent up to the Mount of Olives which is described in Zechariah 14.*"[69]

Some teach that Zechariah 14:4 identifies the place where Christ descends down to at His Second Coming. If they are correct then, Christ would come to the Mount of Olives before He goes to Bozrah in Isaiah 34 and 63. However, the verse informs that His feet stand there, rather than He descends there. Thus, I don't believe this is His first stop at His Second Coming.

Below is presently my personal non-dogmatic view of Zechariah 14:1-5.

Zechariah 14:1-2 identifies the rape, pillaging and plundering of Jerusalem by the Armageddonites around the midpoint of the Tribulation Period. This is where and when the Jewish genocide crusade starts.

Then Zechariah 12:3 points out that as a result of this genocidal campaign, "*Then the Lord will go forth And fight against those nations, As He fights in the day of battle.*" This prophecy gets fulfilled at the Second Coming about three and one-half years after the Jewish genocide has started.

After the actual fighting is completed that fulfills Zechariah 12:3, then Zechariah 14:4 happens and Christ's *"feet will stand on the Mount of Olives."*

Zechariah 14:4-5 is where it gets difficult to interpret. On the surface it appears that while Christ is standing on the Mount of Olives there occurs a great earthquake that splits the Mount of Olives in two, *"making* a very large valley." Of course, Christ is sure-footed and is able to escape injury during such a large quake, which would probably measure as a 10 on the Richter scale, but that seems awkward.

However, it doesn't specifically state that the earthquake happens at the precise time that His feet stand on the Mount, rather it says, *"and the Mount of Olives shall be split in two."* This could imply that by the time His feet stand on the Mount, that the earthquake had already happened and all the rubble and damage is not an obstacle to His victory ascent.

There are at least three major earthquakes that seemingly take place in Israel prior to this point in time. One happens in Israel as part of Ezekiel 38, which likely happens just prior to the start of the Tribulation Period. This account below is about a great earthquake, which causes mountains to be thrown down, steep places to fall and walls to fall to the ground. This could certainly cause the Mount of Olives to split in two.

> "For in My jealousy *and* in the fire of My wrath I have spoken: 'Surely in that day there shall be a great earthquake in the land of Israel, so that the fish of the sea, the birds of the heavens, the beasts of the field, all creeping things that creep on the earth, and all men who *are* on the face of the earth shall shake at My presence. The mountains shall be thrown down, the steep places shall fall, and every wall shall fall to the ground.'
> (Ezek. 38:19-20)

The second one is the terrible earthquake that destroys a tenth of the city of Jerusalem. This devastating quake happens in the same hour that the Two Witnesses, who are identified in Revelation 11:3-12, resurrect and ascend up to heaven. This earthquake happens at the midpoint of the Tribulation Period.

> "In the same hour there was a great earthquake, and a tenth of the city fell. In the earthquake seven thousand people were killed, and the rest were afraid and gave glory to the God of heaven."
> (Rev. 11:13)

The third earthquake is even bigger than the first two and it happens at the end of the Tribulation Period just prior to the Second Coming. This earthquake results from the Seventh Bowl Judgment and it causes mountains to disappear. It also divides the great city into three parts. Some say this city is Jerusalem, while others believe it's the great city of Revelation 18:18.

> "And there were noises and thunderings and lightnings; and there was a great earthquake, such a mighty and great earthquake as had not occurred since men were on the earth. Now the great city was divided into three parts, and the cities of the nations fell. And great Babylon was remembered before God, to give her the cup of the wine of the fierceness of His wrath. Then every island fled away, and the mountains were not found."
> (Rev. 16:18-20)

It's my suspicion that one of these three prior earthquakes is what splits the Mount of Olives in two. Thus, Christ doesn't have to do a balancing act during a major earthquake on the Mount of Olives while standing there.

Zechariah then points out that the large valley that resulted from the prior earthquake will be a pathway of escape for the Jewish remnant when the genocide begins in Jerusalem.

> "You, (*the Jewish remnant*) will run away through my mountain valley, because the valley of the mountains will extend as far as Azal. You will flee, as you, (*your ancestors*), fled from the earthquake during the reign of King Uzziah of Judah. And so the LORD my God will come, and all his holy ones will be accompanying you."
> (Zechariah 14:5, ISV; emphasis added)

This verse instructs the Jewish remnant in Jerusalem to flee through the valley to survive and concludes with the promise that the LORD Jesus Christ will return with His angels and saints from heaven to accompany the Jewish remnant upon their return to Jerusalem.

It's my opinion that one of the first two earthquakes will be the one that splits the Mount of Olives in two. This is because they both happen either prior to, or at the midpoint of, the Tribulation Period. The valley that results from the quake is likely the one that Jews in Jerusalem flee through in Zech. 14:5. The valley needs to exist before the middle of the Tribulation Period.

Revisiting Zechariah 14:2 notice that it ends with this promise, "*Half of the city* (Jerusalem) *shall go into captivity, But the remnant of the people shall not be cut off from the city.*" This Jewish remnant will wisely flee through the valley previously created by the great earthquake to the mountain refuge in Petra. Therefore, they will not be cut off from the city permanently, but will return with Jesus Christ on His Victory Ascent to the Mount of Olives.

19

The Second War of Magog

This chapter reveals the final future war prophecy. After the Battle of Armageddon, the world experiences a thousand years of peace during the millennial reign of Jesus Christ. This is according to Isaiah 2:4 and Micah 4:3, which both foretell,

> "He shall judge between many peoples, And rebuke strong nations afar off; They shall beat their swords into plowshares, And their spears into pruning hooks; Nation shall not lift up sword against nation, Neither shall they learn war anymore."

He refers to the Messiah Jesus Christ. He will have to judge between many peoples and rebuke strong nations afar off, but these nations won't wage war anymore. There appear to be three primary reasons that the Millennium will be void of wars.

1. Isaiah and Micah point out that all of the world's swords and spears, which represent weapons of warfare, will be converted into agricultural tools, such as plowshares and pruning hooks.

2. Jesus Christ will rule the nations with a rod of iron, which will keep them in line. This is taught in Psalm 2:9, Rev. 19:14 and the verse below.

> "He shall rule them, *(the nations),* with a rod of iron; They shall be dashed to pieces like the potter's vessels'" (Rev. 2:27, NKJV; emphasis added)

3. Satan will be unable to sway the nations any longer because he will be confined throughout the Millennium in his fifth abode of the Abyss, which is also called the Bottomless Pit.

> "Then I saw an angel coming down from heaven, having the key to the bottomless pit and a great chain in his hand. He laid hold of the dragon, that serpent of old, who is *the* Devil and Satan, and bound him for a thousand years; and he cast him into the bottomless pit, and shut him up, and set a seal on him, so that he should deceive the nations no more till the thousand years were finished. But after these things he must be released for a little while." (Rev. 20:1-3)

However, observe the caveat in the last verse above that announces, "*But after these things he must be released for a little while.*" The next passage tells us why Satan gets released.

> "Now when the thousand years have expired, Satan will be released from his prison and will go out to deceive the nations which are in the four corners of the earth, Gog and Magog, to gather them together to battle, whose number *is* as the sand of the sea. They went up on the breadth of the earth and surrounded the camp of the saints and the beloved city. And fire came down from God out of heaven and devoured them. The devil, who deceived them, was cast into the lake of fire and brimstone where the beast and the false prophet *are*. And they will be tormented day and night forever and ever." (Rev. 20:7-10)

There are three reasons for Satan's release.

1. To prove that he was, is and will always be a deceiver. Even one-thousand years in "*his prison*" couldn't persuade him to change his evil ways.

2. To lead a final rebellion of all the world's sinners who were tired of being ruled by Jesus Christ's rod of iron. Yes, there will still be a sin-nature in the Millennium. Isaiah the prophet tells us this. In the verse below we discover that in the Millennium there is an age of accountability. Everyone

born during that period will have one hundred years to make a decision to receive Jesus Christ as their Savior.

> "No more shall an infant from there *live but a few* days, Nor an old man who has not fulfilled his days; For the child shall die one hundred years old, But the sinner *being* one hundred years old shall be accursed."
> (Isaiah 65:20)

This means, that unlike today, those who commit a sin in the Millennium will not be able to use the excuse that, "*the Devil made me do it,*" because the Devil will be chained up in the Abyss.

3. To send Satan into his seventh and final abode, the Lake of Fire.

This final future war prophecy happens after "*the thousand years have expired.*" At that time, Satan will travel to "*the four corners of the earth*" and assemble a massive international army, "*whose number is as the sand of the sea.*" They are going to deploy to the "*beloved city*" of Jerusalem. Jerusalem is where the KING OF KINGS and LORD OF LORDS, with His rod of iron, will be hailing from.

> "At that time Jerusalem shall be called The Throne of the Lord, and all the nations shall be gathered to it, to the name of the Lord, to Jerusalem. No more shall they follow the dictates of their evil hearts." (Jeremiah 3:17)

During the Millennium, the nations will gather to Jerusalem to pay homage to Jesus Christ and "*No more shall they follow the dictates of their evil hearts.*" However after the Millennium, Satan will surround the beloved city with the rebels who choose to "*follow the dictates of their evil hearts.*"

Somehow, Satan is able to influence these deluded troops into thinking that they can fist fight and fireball their way to freedom from the rod of iron. Unless they can reconvert the plowshares and pruning forks back into swords and spears and also learn how to make war, they won't have useful weapons nor know how to fight this final battle.

Moreover, how do they deploy from the four corners of the earth to their destination in Jerusalem? Will there be planes, trains and automobiles at that time? Will they be arriving as a cavalry of horsemen and foot soldiers? Will they even have protective helmets and matching uniforms? How will Satan suit them up for his last stand? It's all a moot point, because no sooner do they arrive until the "*fire came down from God out of heaven and devoured them.*"

Comparing the Two Magog Invasions

Some teach that the Magog invasion identified in Ezekiel 38 is the same as the one in Revelation 20:7-10. However, there are several distinct differences between these two biblical predictions. Some of these dissimilarities are provided below.

- *The battlefields*: Ezek. 39:2; 38:16 takes place on the mountains of Israel, but Rev. 20:9 says the troops surround the camp of the saints and the beloved city of Jerusalem.
- *The defeats*: Ezek. 38:19-22 predicts a great earthquake, every man's sword will be against his brother, pestilence and bloodshed, flooding rain, great hailstones, fire, and brimstone. In Rev. 20:9 only fire comes down from God out of heaven.
- *The troops*: Ezek. 38:2-7 identifies a limited group of localized Muslim nations led by Russia that invade from the north. Rev. 20:8 speaks of an international army, whose number is as the sand of the sea, from nations which are in the four quarters of the earth.
- *The weapons of warfare*: Ezek. 39:9-10 says that Israel will be burning the enemies' weapons for seven years. According to Isaiah 2:4 and Micah 4:3, the weapons that used to exist in the old earth have since been destroyed and turned

into farm implements, (plowshares and pruning hooks). It hardly seems that Israel will be able to burn weapons that apparently no longer exist.

- *The timing of the weapons' burning*: Ezek. 39:9 emphasizes the weapons supply can provide fuel to burn for seven years, but shortly after the Rev. 20:7-10 Magog prophecy concludes, the White Throne Judgment happens in Rev. 20:11-15 and then the Eternal Order starts in Rev. 21 and 22. It seems unlikely that weapons will be burning in these two aftermath scenarios.

- *The timing of Israel's rebirth vs. the reign of Jesus Christ*: Ezek. 38:8 points out that the Gog of Magog invasion takes place shortly after the Jews are restored to their homeland Israel. Rev. 20:7 says that Satan is loosed after Jesus the Messiah has reigned over the world for one thousand years.

- *The timing of the regathering of Israel*: Ezek. 38:8 points out that the Jews are regathered from the nations to Israel. In the Millennium, there is no hint of an additional Jewish dispersion that would require another regathering. Thus, Rev. 20:7-10 happens over one thousand years after Israel had been regathered.

- *The leaders of the invasions*: Ezek. 38:2-11 says it's Gog of Magog, but in Revelation 20:7-8 it's clearly Satan released from the abyss.

Some of these comparisons above were taken from the book entitled, *Northern Storm Rising: Russia, Iran, and the Emerging End-Times Military Coalition Against Israel,* by Dr. Ron Rhodes. I highly recommend this book for those who want to gain a better understanding of the prophecies found in Ezekiel 38 and 39.

Conclusion

As has been the case with several of the prophetic wars identified within this book, the LORD intervenes to win this war. This final war serves the purposes of purging the rebels from the earth and eliminating Satan from all future activities involving God's people. Shortly after this war the Eternal Order commences and it will be characterized, not by war, but by the following.

> "Now I saw a new heaven and a new earth, for the first heaven and the first earth had passed away. Also there was no more sea. Then I, John, saw the holy city, New Jerusalem, coming down out of heaven from God, prepared as a bride adorned for her husband. And I heard a loud voice from heaven saying, "Behold, the tabernacle of God *is* with men, and He will dwell with them, and they shall be His people. God Himself will be with them *and be* their God. And God will wipe away every tear from their eyes; there shall be no more death, nor sorrow, nor crying. There shall be no more pain, for the former things, (*including wars*), have passed away."
> (Revelation 22:1-4, NKJV; emphasis added)

The End…

Appendices

Appendix 1:

Why the Destruction of Damascus is a Future War Prophecy

(Research done by Brad Myers)

Isaiah 17:1 predicts that Damascus will be utterly destroyed as a city someday. The literal interpretation of the verse reads that the city will be reduced to a ruinous heap of rubble. Damascus is thought to be one of the oldest continuously inhabited cities in history, dating back over four thousand years ago to the time of the Hebrew patriarch Abraham. It is the capital city of Syria.

> The oracle concerning Damascus. "Behold,
> Damascus is about to be removed from
> being a city And will become a fallen ruin."
> (Isaiah 17:1, NASB 1995)

Dr. Charles Dyer, Dr. Mark Hitchcock and Dr. Andy Woods are by far the loudest voices promoting the biblical interpretation that all of the prophecies in Isaiah 17:1-14 and Jeremiah 49:23-27 have already been fulfilled in history.

The Christian Post published a piece on their website by Christian Post contributor, Anugrah Kumar titled, "*1 in 3 Americans Link Syrian Conflict to Bible's End-Time Prophecy Survey Finds.*" Kumar ends his report with the words of Charles Dyer professor at Moody Bible Institute:

> *"Dr. Charlie Dyer, professor at Moody Bible Institute in Chicago, recently told Chicago Sun-Times that Damascus was destroyed in the 7th and 8th centuries."*

> *"Isaiah 17 predicted the destruction of the city, along with the*

> *destruction of the northern kingdom of Israel...Damascus was captured by Assyrians in 732 BC and the northern kingdom of Israel fell when the capital city of Samaria was captured by the Assyrians in 722 BC."*
>
> *"And 100 years later, the prophet Jeremiah also predicted the fall of Damascus, which had been rebuilt."*
>
> Dyer added. *"His message was fulfilled when the city was captured by Nebuchadnezzar of Babylon."* [70]

John Ankerberg on his website posts the article, *"Has The Destruction of Damascus Been Fulfilled?"* In the article he quotes the words of prophecy expert Dr. Mark Hitchcock.

> *"I believe it makes more sense to hold that Isaiah 17 was fulfilled in the eighth century BC when both Damascus, the capital of Syria, and Samaria, the capital of Israel, were hammered by the Assyrians. In that conquest, both Damascus and Samaria were destroyed, just as Isaiah 17 predicts. According to history, Tiglath-pileser III (745–727 BC) pushed vigorously to the west, and in 734 the Assyrians advanced and laid siege to Damascus, which fell two years later in 732. In other words, we don't need to look for the fulfillment of Isaiah 17 today because it has already occurred—taking place in 732 BC."* [71]

Dr. Andy Woods earned a Master of Theology degree with High Honors and a Doctor of Philosophy in Bible Exposition at Dallas Theological Seminary and now serves as President of Chafer Theological Seminary and senior pastor of Sugar Land Bible Church. He is author of the books: *"The Middle East Meltdown: The Coming Islamic Invasion of Israel"* and *"Babylon: The Bookends of Prophetic History."*

Dr. Woods did an extensive teaching on Isaiah 17 and Jeremiah 49 concerning Damascus as Sr. Pastor of Sugar Land Bible Church in Texas. This teaching can be seen on his YouTube channel. His teaching on Damascus can be viewed by watching The Middle East Meltdown videos 27, 28 and 29.

Dr. Woods wanted everyone to know that he got his information on Damascus from the book "Showdown with Iran" by Dr. Mark Hitchcock in which he said, *"I'm sort of indebted to him for his research."*

The following are the words of pastor and teacher Dr. Andy Woods that can be heard watching his videos. The excerpts below are taken from the video transcripts.

The Middle East Meltdown video #29, 9/4/22:

…"yes Damascus is about to be removed from being a city at the time Isaiah wrote that in the 7th century so this is actually a prophecy or the eighth century I should say this is a prophecy that actually has already been fulfilled in 732 BC 700 years before the time of Christ when Tiglath-Pileser of Assyria came and destroyed Damascus and Syria …" [72]

The Middle East Meltdown video #28, 8/28/22:

…"and so people… say well Syria must have some sort of major role in the end times there are basically two passages that they gravitate towards to prove this and it seems to fit because it fits with the newspaper, one is in Isaiah 17 verses 1 and 2… the second one is in Jeremiah 49 verses 23 through 27." [73]

The Middle East Meltdown video #27, 8/21/22:

…"a lot of these guys I agree with on so many things but what they're doing in my opinion is they're pushing the envelope on Isaiah 17 and trying to make Isaiah 17 say something that it really isn't saying in order to build their very exciting prophetic scenario…what I'm going to say here is this prophecy happened already in 732 B.C. when Damascus was destroyed by Tiglath-Pileser of Assyria and this is how dispensationalists, our camp, has traditionally understood this prophecy…" [74]

The Middle East Meltdown video #29, 9/4/22

...*"they're hyping prophecies into some kind of newspaper scenario. When you carefully look at those prophecies the prophecies don't support what it is they're saying and so there's people out there that will start not with the Bible but they'll start with the newspaper and read that back into the Bible when the Bible really doesn't support what it is they're saying and these are people that are generally well-intentioned but they haven't been in my opinion taught very well...If I don't mention who they are you're not going to recognize the false teaching when it shows up......if I don't mention the names of people within the Evangelical camp, how in the world could you have any red flags about people concerning false teachings and the most destructive forms of false teaching are not false teachings that come from outside the church and come in. Paul over and over again warns about heresies coming up within the church ......if you're actually a legitimate pastor, part of that responsibility involves the need to call out the names of people that are throwing the body of Christ into a state of confusion."* [75]

Dr. Andy Woods explains how we should interpret Jeremiah 49:23-27. He quotes from his professor Charles Dyer, in the "Bible Knowledge Commentary" which included Dyer's interpretation of Jeremiah 49:23-27.

The Middle East Meltdown video #29, 9/4/22:

...*"so what do we do then with Jeremiah 49 verses 23-27. Well here is my professor who I think has it right. Charles Dyer in the Bible Knowledge Commentary and this is what he says concerning the prophecy of the destruction of Damascus found in Jeremiah 49:23-27. He says three of the major cities of Syria: Hamath, Arpad and Damascus were dismayed because of the bad news of Babylon's advance, so this is something that actually took place in the sixth, seventh centuries roughly. Damascus's pain was like that of a woman in labor and then he says this in Nebuchadnezzar's attack on Damascus in other words according to Charles Dyer, Jeremiah 49 verses 23-27 is not some kind of prophecy about the imminent destruction of Damascus what it's about, is something Nebuchadnezzar did to Damascus back in the time of Jeremiah and Jeremiah is just making a short-term prediction in Nebuchadnezzar's attack on Damascus..."* [76]

The Middle East Meltdown video #29, 9/4/22

..."so nobody today is saying okay we're going to book a trip to the Middle East and we're going to go see the towers of Ben Haddad because that's something that's long gone. This is a prophecy that was fulfilled a long time ago so when you actually look at Isaiah 17 and Jeremiah 49 which are the two passages that Joel Rosenberg is using amongst other interpreters to build this scenario, what you see is those passages do not support what he is saying. The Bible is very clear that we are not to add or take away from God's book just read what He says at the end of the Book of Revelation chapter 22 and the harshness that He announces on people that will manipulate His Word, if you take away I'll take away your name from The Book of Life. That sounds pretty serious to me if you add to My Word I will add to you the curses that are in this book. It looks pretty serious to me ... even though this false teaching is coming from people that generally I like and agree with you. Now the Bible never says don't call out false teachings except if it's one of your friends." [77]

These above statements by Pastor Andy Woods of Sugar Land Bible Church should be taken very seriously by the following Bible teachers: Bill Salus, Joel Rosenberg, Britt Gillette, Harry Ironside, Harry Bultema, Dr. Arnold Fruchtenbaum, Hal Lindsey, Dr. Vernon McGee, Dr. David Hocking, Ray Steadman, Dr. Chuck Missler, Jon Courson, Ray Bentley, Jack Hibbs, Dr. David Reagan, Nathan Jones, Amir Tsarfati, Tom Hughes, Gary Stearman, Mondo Gonzales, J.D. Farag, Todd Hampton, Brett Meador, Jack Kelly, Daymond Duck, Terry James, Dr. Thomas Ice, Jan Markell, Barry Stagner, Brandon Holthaus and many others.

This is only a sample number of conservative dispensationalists who believe that the passages in Isaiah 17 and Jeremiah 49, concerning Damascus most likely still awaits fulfillment in the future.

Are these Bible teachers generally well-intentioned but they haven't been taught very well?

Are these Bible teachers who simply have a different interpretation of Isaiah 17:1-14 and Jeremiah 49:23-27 guilty of spreading false teachings and heresies which is throwing the body of Christ into a state of confusion?

Are these Bible teachers spreading false teaching and manipulating God's word so seriously God may add to them the curses in the Book of Revelation and take their name from The Book of Life in Revelation 22:18-19?

> "An oracle concerning Damascus. "Behold, Damascus will cease to be a city and will become a heap of ruins.""
> (Isaiah 17:1, ESV)

Notice that the biblical text does not simply say Damascus will cease as a city and be destroyed. It says the city of Damascus will become a heap of ruins. In world history armies have destroyed cities without destroying ALL the buildings in which people live.

Many Christians cite Smith's Bible Dictionary and Easton's Bible Dictionary as historical proof that the city of Damascus was destroyed by the Assyrians as the Bible foretold in Isaiah 17:1.

Smith's Bible Dictionary:

"Under Ahaz it was taken by Tiglath-pileser (2 Kings 16:7-9) the kingdom of Damascus brought to an end, and the city itself destroyed, the inhabitants being carried captive into Assyria..." [78]

Easton's Bible Dictionary:

"The Syrians were at length subdued by the Assyrians, the city of Damascus was taken and destroyed, and the inhabitants carried captive into Assyria..." [79]

According to Smith's Bible Dictionary and Easton's Bible Dictionary one can say that the city of Damascus was destroyed by the Assyrians, by Assyrian king Tiglath-Pileser III, but was the city of Damascus in 732 B.C. actually reduced to RUINS as worded by an overwhelming number of Bible translations of Isaiah 17:1?

In the Bible we read in 2 Kings 16:9-10 the biblical account of when the king of Assyria, Tiglath-Pileser went against Damascus and captured it.

> "... the king of Assyria went up AGAINST DAMASCUS and CAPTURED IT, and carried the people of it away into exile to Kir, and put Rezin to death. Now King Ahaz WENT TO DAMASCUS to meet TIGLATH-PILESER king of Assyria, and saw the altar which was AT DAMASCUS; and King Ahaz sent to Urijah the priest the pattern of the altar and its model, according to all its workmanship."
> (2 Kings 16:9-10, NASB 1995)

As you can see the biblical account has no record of Tiglath-Pileser attacking Damascus and the city becoming a heap of ruins. If the city of Damascus was in ruins after the destruction, how was King Ahaz still able to meet TIGLATH-PILESER IN A CITY that the Assyrians literally reduced to rubble?

Here are two separate historical accounts that seem to be very strong evidence that the city of Damascus WAS NOT removed from being a city and became a heap of ruins when the Assyrians attacked in 732 B.C.

Tyndale Bible Dictionary, page 346:

> *"The Assyrian king Tiglath-pileser III ("Pul") agreed and marched against the Syro-Israelite confederation. After defeating Israel, he attacked Damascus, plundered the city, deported the population, and replaced them with foreigners from other captured lands. Damascus was no longer an independent city-state.*

Due to its key location, Damascus remained important, and the Assyrians used the city as a provincial capital." [80]

The biblical text in Isaiah 17:1 is clearly saying "Damascus is about to be removed from being a city and will become a fallen ruin." This seems to suggest strongly that the city of Damascus is removed from being a city because of the utter devastation that results in the city becoming a fallen ruin.

Since this is the case it does not seem to make sense that the Assyrians deported the population and replaced them with foreigners in a city that has been reduced to ruins. In addition, how can the Assyrians use the city of Damascus as a provincial capital when it is a fallen ruin? Most importantly, there is no historical evidence that the Assyrians in 732 B.C. had to totally rebuild the city of Damascus after it had become a fallen ruin before moving in people to live there again.

In this second historical account, George Smith who worked in the Assyriology Department of the British Museum and a world-renowned expert on the history of the Assyrians authored a book in 1876 entitled, *"Ancient History from the Monuments: Assyria from the Earliest Times to the Fall of Nineveh"* explains on pages 87-88 what took place historically to the city of Damascus.

"Tiglath-Pileser now led his army to Damascus, after crucifying the captains of the Syrian army who had fallen into his hand and closely invested the Syrian capital. Tiglath-Pileser tells us that he shut up Rezon in Damascus like a caged bird, and cut down all the fine forests around the city for use in the siege, not leaving a single tree near the capital. Several places round were spoiled, and sixteen districts of Damascus were destroyed like a flood ...591 cities were captured and spoiled, and the whole of the kingdom of Rezon subdued. Damascus, however held out, and could only be reduced by famine, so leaving part of his army before the city, Tiglath-Pileser marched against the other rebels." [81]

Notice that the famous historian on the history of the Assyrians said, "sixteen districts of Damascus were destroyed like a flood ... DAMASCUS HOWEVER HELD OUT, and could ONLY BE REDUCED BY FAMINE." He is obviously saying that the sixteen districts of Damascus that were destroyed like a flood are not what took place to the actual capital city of Damascus and this would also mean that the city of Damascus was not destroyed like the ruins from the flood either.

The Moody Bible Commentary on page 1031 certainly did not believe that Tiglath- Pileser III's conquest destroyed the city of Damascus like ruins from the flood when it states:

"Tiglath- pileser 111's conquest would be a mere foreshadowing of a far more serious conquest at the end of days."

Did conservative Bible scholars Dr. Charles J. Ellicott, Dr. Arno Gaebelein and Dr. J. Dwight Pentecost believe that the prophecy in Isaiah 17 already happened in 732 B.C. when Damascus was destroyed by Tiglath-Pileser of Assyria?

Dr. Charles J. Ellicott, conservative scholar and author of "Ellicott's Bible Commentary for English Readers" published in 1905 said in his commentary on Isaiah 17:1: "Writing probably early in the reign of Hezekiah, Isaiah now looks forward to a further fulfillment in the future."

"The burden of Damascus.—Syria, it will be remembered, had been "confederate with Ephraim," i.e., with the kingdom of Israel, against Judah in the reign of Ahaz, and the prophet had then foretold its overthrow by Assyria (Isaiah 7:1-16). In 2 Kings 16:9, 2 Chron. 28:29, we have a partial fulfillment of that prediction. Writing probably early in the reign of Hezekiah, Isaiah now looks forward to a further fulfillment in the future."
[82]

Dr. Arno Gaebelein, author of the "Annotated Bible" published in 1922 states that "Tiglath-pileser, King of Assyria, executed the judgment upon Damascus and made of it a ruinous heap. BUT the judgment is ALSO FUTURE."

> "*Damascus to be a ruinous heap (Isaiah 17:1-3) Judgment upon Ephraim (Isaiah 17:4-11) Woe to the enemies of Israel (Isaiah 17:12-14) Damascus was the ancient city of Syria, mentioned for the first time in Genesis 15:1-21. Syria and Ephraim had made common cause against the house of David. Tiglath-pileser, King of Assyria, executed the judgment upon Damascus and made of it a ruinous heap. But the judgment is also future. And the enemies of Israel, which trouble His people, will be troubled "in that day." It is a solemn word with which this chapter closes, "This is the portion of them that spoil us, and the lot of them that rob us.*" [83]

Dr. J. Dwight Pentecost taught 58 years at Dallas Theological Seminary and was the author of the highly successful book "Things To Come" published in 1958. On page 264 he wrote the following words concerning Damascus in Isaiah 17:1-4 and Jeremiah 49:23-27.

> "*There is a divine program for the Gentile nations that is to come to fulfillment in the tribulation period....*"

> "*The Judgments upon Nations Adjacent to Israel.... These predictions are set forth in various portions of the Old Testament... Damascus (Isa. 17:1-14; Jer. 49:23-27)...*" [84]

Did Dr. Charles J. Ellicott in the late 1800's, Dr. Arno Gaebelein in the 1920's, and Dr. J. Dwight Pentecost in the 1950's start with their newspaper and read back into the Bible what the Bible really doesn't say to support their biblical interpretation? Do their words suggest that there is a possibility that Isaiah 17 and Jeremiah 49, concerning the city of Damascus was removed from being a city and became a heap of ruins in 732 B.C.?

Is it highly possible that these Christians and many others during the course of church history simply looked at the historical accounts of what took place in 732 B.C. concerning the city of Damascus and compared that with the biblical texts and came to the conclusion that somehow there are prophecies that are still awaiting further fulfillment in the future?

Dr. Mark Hitchcock, Dr. Andy Woods along with Dr. Charles Dyer all believe the prophet Jeremiah predicted in Jeremiah 49:23-27 the fall of Damascus and his message was fulfilled when the city was captured by Nebuchadnezzar of Babylon.

Read what Dr. John Walvoord says about the events of Jeremiah 49:23-27 regarding Damascus in his best-selling book *"Every Prophecy of the Bible"* on pages 150-151 that was published in 1999.

Dr. John Walvoord:

"Jeremiah 49:23-27. Damascus, one of the oldest cities in the Middle East, was described here as being destroyed by fire. It was first mentioned in Scripture in Genesis 14:15 and continued to be an important city throughout biblical history. THOUGH DESTROYED by the ASSYRIANS, it was later rebuilt BEFORE JEREMIAH's TIME. HERE IT WAS DESTROYED ONCE AGAIN. Its DESTRUCTION HERE prophesied in Jeremiah WAS PREDICTED ALSO IN ISAIAH 7:8, 8:4; 17:1-3. In New Testament times it again was a flourishing city. The home of Ananias in Damascus, referred to as "the city of renown" (Jer. 49:25), was described here as suffering defeat of its soldiers and fire on its walls." [85]

It is really interesting that Dr. John Walvoord, the former president at Dallas Theological Seminary looked specifically at Jeremiah 49:23-27 and did not give his interpretation on what time in history these events actually occurred.

In his online commentary on Jeremiah 49:26-27, Pastor David Guzik author of the *"Enduring Word Bible Commentary"* provides a very important quote by Bible scholar Charles L. Feinberg on the biblical meaning of *"all the men of war shall be cut off in that day, says the Lord of Hosts, I will kindle a fire in the wall of Damascus and it shall consume the palaces of Ben-Hadad."*

Charles Feinberg, a professor of the Old Testament at Dallas Theological Seminary states these shocking words:

"Perhaps the greatest fulfillment of this is still in the future." "Expositors have difficulty fitting this prophecy into any recorded event related to Damascus." [86]

Incredibly, Feinberg believes that perhaps the GREATEST fulfillment of the burning of the palaces of Ben-Hadad is STILL IN THE FUTURE, which is the belief of those Bible teachers who, according to Dr. Andy Woods, are *"spreading false teaching and throwing the body of Christ into confusion"* when they say that the events of Jeremiah 49 about Damascus is still in the future.

Why would Bible expositors have difficulty fitting this prophecy into any recorded event in history related to Damascus in Jeremiah 49:26-27? Could it be simply because those events are still to play out in the future?

Dr. Andy Woods over the years has recommended many times that Christians read Dr. John Walvoord's excellent book *"Every Prophecy of the Bible"* that was published in 1999. In this book Dr. Walvoord gives his interpretation on the prophecies found in Jeremiah 49 concerning Ammon, Edom, Damascus, Kedar and Hazor, and Elam. On page 151 speaking about Elam's destruction in verses 34-38, Dr. Walvoord believes the complete destruction of Elam within the country of Iran does not seem to have been fulfilled in history.

Dr. John Walvoord:

"Jeremiah 49:34-39. The prophecy concerning Elam referred to an area east of Babylon, known today as Iran. The destruction of Elam was described as breaking her bow, for, like Kedar, Elam was noted for archery. The complete destruction of Elam does

not seem to have been fulfilled in history and may have its final chapter in the future in connection with the judgments at the second coming of Christ. Elam was promised, however, restoration (v 39)." [87]

Since the complete destruction of Elam in Iran, (Jeremiah 49:34-39) does not seem to have been fulfilled in history according to Dr. John Walvoord, could the same thing be said of Damascus in chapter 49:23-27?

Appendix 2:

Why Psalm 83 is a Prayer and a Future War Prophecy

(Research done by Brad Myers)

This appendix serves as an extension to the chapter entitled, "Psalm 83: The Final Arab-Israeli War." It was identified under the subsection of that chapter called the "The Psalm 83 Objections." It will explain why this author, as well as others who will be noted, believe that Psalm 83 is more than a prayer, but is an actual Bible prophecy, and that it remains unfulfilled.

Is Psalm 83 Only a Prayer?

Some believe that Psalm 83 is not a prophecy, but is only an imprecatory prayer, in which Asaph petitions the LORD to intervene on behalf of Israel to eliminate their general enemies. Dr. Thomas Ice, Executive Director of the Pre-Trib Research Center quotes prophecy expert Mark Hitchcock on why Psalm 83 should not be a war prophecy of the last days.

> *"It may be that constructing a separate end time war out of Psalm 83 is reading too much into a text that is simply saying that Israel has been and always will be surrounded by enemies and that someday the Lord will finally deal with them."* [88]

Dr. Thomas Ice puts forward these strong comments regarding Christians that believe Psalm 83 is a war prophecy of the future.

> *"While I consider Bill Salus and others who take this view to be friends and fellow protagonist within the field of Bible prophecy, however, there comes a time when friends must speak out against a friend when what they teach is not really found in the Bible. This is why I am sounding the alarm concerning the so-called "Psalm 83 war." It is clear to me that Psalm 83 is an imprecatory request on behalf of the nation of Israel by Asaph 3,000 years ago. This is the reason that Psalm 83 is classified as a national lament. There is no prophecy in the Psalm"...*[89]

Senior Pastor Andy Woods presented a teaching on how to correctly interpret Psalm 83 at Sugar Land Bible Church on September 11, 2022. Dr. Andy Woods explains in detail why he feels strongly that Psalm 83 should be considered only as an imprecatory prayer not a war prophecy in the future. You can watch this teaching on his YouTube channel by listening to The Middle East Meltdown video.

The Middle East Meltdown video #30, 9/11/21

(These excerpts are taken from the video transcript)

> *"Psalm 83 does not contain the language of predictive prophecy it's just a prayer of an imprecatory nature Asaph you know looks out at the nations that keep bothering Israel and he's just praying Lord in the end I hope you sock it to him um he's not making any kind of independent prediction... Psalm 83 is not a war or a prediction about a war as we read Psalm 83. There is no war or battle found in Psalm 83. I mean to me that's problematic everybody's talking about the Psalm 83 war I read through that I didn't see any war did you?..."*

> *"At some point in your ministry you have to figure out what you're more interested in. Are you interested in selling books or are you interested in giving an account to God? As a teacher*

> when the Book of James chapter 3 verse 1 says let few of you presume to be teachers knowing that the teacher must give a stricter accounting to God that's what I'm thinking about I'm not thinking about popularity, book sales, sensationalistic type speaking etc."

> "Psalm 83 is Asaph back in 950 BC mentioning in his prayer various nations that were bothering Israel back in 950 BC and he's praying a prayer of imprecation and he's basically saying Lord I hope you take these countries out one day he's not making a prediction about a war he's not making a forecast about a war he's praying a prayer of imprecation which is kind of common in the Psalms."

> "I (Dr. Woods) think Psalm 83 is not a war is because if you and this is the where the genre sensitivity comes in if you start taking things in the Bible that are designed to be imprecatory prayers and carte blanche converting them into prophecies then that opens up Pandora's Box because if you do it with this prayer this imprecatory prayer then there's a ton of other imprecatory prayers in the Psalms and suddenly you got to start converting those into prophecies also let me show you how common in the psalter these prayer these imprecatory prayers are."

> "So if you're going to take Psalm 83 and you're going to make that a prophecy then you've got to create independent wars for all of these. The Psalm 6:10 war, Psalm 7:6 war, Psalm 25:2 war, Psalm 25:19 war, Psalm 31:15 war, Psalm 56:2 war Psalm 56:9 war, Psalm 69:18 war and Psalm 102:8."[90]

So my question to Dr. Woods is, why would we have to take the personal enemies of David throughout these specific psalms and create independent war prophecies about nations that want to go to wipe out the nation of Israel? Look at these Psalms verses below that Woods cites. They are all dealing with enemies of David, not with the destruction of Israel.

"All MY ENEMIES will be ashamed and greatly dismayed;
They shall turn back, they will suddenly be ashamed."
(Psalm 6:10, NASB 1995; emphasis added)

"Arise, O LORD, in your anger; lift yourself up against
the fury of MY ENEMIES; awake for ME; you have
appointed a judgment."
(Psalm 7:6, ESV; emphasis added)

"O my God, in You I trust, Do not let ME be ashamed;
Do not let MY ENEMIES exult over ME
(Psalm 25:2, NASB 1995; emphasis added)

"Look upon MY ENEMIES, for they are many, And
they HATE ME with violent hatred.
(Psalm 25:19, NASB 1995; emphasis added)

"MY times are in Your hand; Deliver ME from the hand
of MY ENEMIES and from those who persecute ME."
(Psalm 31:15, NASB 1995; emphasis added)

"MY FOES have trampled upon ME all day long, For
they are many who fight proudly AGAINST ME."
(Psalm 56:2, NASB 1995; emphasis added)

"Then MY ENEMIES will turn back in the day when I
CALL; This I KNOW, that God is FOR ME."
(Psalm 56:9, NASB 1995; emphasis added)

"Oh draw near to MY SOUL and redeem it; Ransom me
because of MY ENEMIES!"
(Psalm 69:18, NASB 1995; emphasis added)

"MY ENEMIES have reproached ME all day long; Those
who DERIDE ME have used MY NAME as a curse."
(Psalm 102:8, NASB 1995; emphasis added)

Did you notice all THESE ENEMIES are targeting DAVID and not nations threatening to wipe out Israel as a nation? Is comparing the personal ENEMIES of DAVID that want to harm or kill him in these psalms the same as comparing the enemies in Psalm 83 that want to wipe out Israel from existence? If Psalm 83 is simply a prayer for the Lord to someday deal with the hostile enemies that surround the nation of Israel, why is there so much tremendous detail about ten specific hostile enemies that form into an Arab confederacy?

Psalm 83 as a Future War Prophecy

In 2017 Dr. David Reagan wrote an article entitled *"Bill Salus, a True Eschatologist."* This piece was featured in the 2017 edition of Lamplighter Magazine. Here is only a sample of the interesting things Dr. Reagan said about Bill's thesis of the Psalm 83 war.

> *"But if anyone could be called an Eschatologist, it would be Bill — and not because he is stuffy. Rather, he brings an inquisitive attitude to God's Prophetic Word, and this attitude propels him to constantly search for end time prophecies that may have been overlooked or misinterpreted…Basically, what he argued was that Psalm 83 is a prophecy about an end time war that is yet to occur – a war between Israel and all the Arab states with whom it shares a common border… Psalm 83 had been considered to be simply a lament over the desire of the nations of the world to destroy Israel. And most Bible prophecy specialists quickly dismissed Bill's thesis as nonsense…"* [91]

Fast forward to May 10, 2023, when Dr. David Reagan states the following in his book entitled, the 9 Wars of the End Times on page 37.

> *"Personally, I have come to the following conclusions:*
>
> - *There is no biblical fulfillment of Psalm 83.*
> - *The complete fulfillment of Psalm 83 is most likely in the future, serving as the event that will bring a brief time of peace to Israel – as well as expanded territory and increased wealth.*
> - *The Psalm 83 War will most likely pave the way for the War of Gog & Magog, probably because the outcome will prompt*

> *Arab nations to call for Russia and its Muslim allies to come to their aid."*

In his Believer's Bible Commentary that was published in 1995, William MacDonald on pages 675-676 gives his interpretation of Psalm 83 which he believes will perhaps have further fulfillments involving enemies that threaten the annihilation of Israel with mostly people who are near relatives of the Israelites. He states:

> *"For many Bible lovers, Psalm 83 took on new meaning after the Six-Day War. And perhaps it will have further fulfillments... The details are true to life. The enemies are in tumult... They threaten the annihilation of Israel... They form a formidable federation of nations- mostly of people who are near relatives of the Israelites...How could little Israel stand against such an overwhelming conspiracy?,,, He sends a victory that defies all human explanations."* [92]

The Anchor Bible Psalms 51-100 by Mitchell Dahood, S.J. in 1968 on page 273 says this about the nations that want to wipe out Israel.

> *"A National lament in which the poet or singer prays on behalf of the nation for deliverance from the surrounding enemies who threaten its existence. History transmits no record of the national crisis when the nations enumerated in this psalm formed a league to wipe out Israel..."* [93]

The New American Commentary Psalms 73-150 on pages 121-123 published in 2019 referencing Psalm 83, informs that the Psalm indicates that Israel is facing an imminent military conspiracy with ten hostile nations joined together in their desire to expunge the memory of Israel forever.

> *"The Psalm indicates that Israel is facing an imminent military conspiracy (vv.3-5 {4-6} by several nations allied against it (vv. 6-8{7-9}. Ten hostile enemies are listed, but there is no time noted in the OT historical narratives when these ten nations joined together against Israel... This is a calculated, sinister plot,*

as the hostile nations conspire to oppose God to inflict collateral damage on God's people. Israel is the battlefield on which this conflict between God and his enemies plays out... 83:4... This verse quotes the words of the enemies as they plot against Israel, encouraging one another to proceed with this dastardly deed. They want to obliterate Israel as a nation. Defeat is not enough; only total devastation will suffice for them. In fact, they collude to expunge the memory of Israel forever. If they were to have their way, Israel would be erased from the roll of nations and from the book of history, as the later agendas of Hamman (Esther 3) and Hitler attempted as well. Had they been successful in OT times, God's plan of redemption ...would have been thwarted. This, then, is a frontal attack on God's world order and sovereign plan for history 83:5... it appears that their intent is to obliterate Israel, but in reality they want to subvert God's program for history." [94]

The New Century Bible Psalms Volume 2 was published in 1972. This Bible commentary weighs in on their interpretation of the events in Psalm 83 which they believe involves the threat of a foreign invasion of 10 national groups or nations which result in calamities for these enemies of Israel. [95]

"This Psalm is a National Lament ... uttered, in the hour of distress, at some service of intercession. The actual calamity is the apparently imminent threat of a foreign invasion, and verses 6-8 list the ten nations involved in this plotting." (Page 595).

"The following verses (6-8) enumerate the peoples taking part in this scheming; the coalition comprises ten nations. As far as our present goes, we do not know of any specific situation in which all the ten national groups were threatening Israel." (Page 597).

"(14-15) The community prays for a complete annihilation of the enemies and the brush fire metaphor for destruction." (Page 600).

"(18) Let them know... the psalmist expects that the calamities of the nations will bring them to their senses and that they will

know or recognize the authority of Yahweh...

the Most High... The nations thought (as implied by their attitude) that they and their gods were the masters of the earth... but the subsequent events will show the real and only Lord is Yahweh, who is in authority above the whole earth." (Page 601).

John Peter Lange is a well-respected theologian who is the author of the Lange Commentary on the Holy Scripture which was published in 1877. He points out that those combined against Israel, are never mentioned elsewhere as enemies allied at the same time and for the purpose of annihilating Israel. Lange notes:

"With regard to the time of composition, the following difficulty meets us. The ten nations who are here enumerated as being combined against Israel, are never mentioned elsewhere as enemies allied at the same time and for the purpose of annihilating Israel." [96]

In addition, John Peter Lange believes there were some individuals during his time that believed the Psalm was just a general idea, that there were enemies from all sides of Israel but Lange believed that the detailed information in Psalm 83:8 is unfavorable to their view of Psalm 83 as just a general idea or prayer. Here is how he explains it:

"And yet the expressions are of such a nature, that we cannot be inclined to consider this enumeration as only a poetical individualizing of the general idea: enemies from all sides (De Wette, Hupfeld). The position of Assyria as an auxiliary of the sons of Lot, that is, of the Moabites and Ammonites, is especially unfavorable to this view." [97]

Conclusion

This appendix presented a strong case that Psalm 83 is a legitimate Bible prophecy that remains unfulfilled. So, more than a prayer it identifies a future war between Israel and the surrounding Arab nations that share common borders with Israel. These very nations, waged war with Israel in 1948 in an attempt to destroy the restored Jewish state, but they were unsuccessful.

As was pointed out in the chapter entitled, "Psalm 83: The Final Arab-Israeli War" under the subsection of that chapter called the "The Psalm 83 Objections," the 1948 war was not the final fulfillment of Psalm 83. That section also explained why Psalm 83 and Ezekiel 38 are not the same war prophecy.

Endnotes

1) J. Barton Payne's information was taken on 2/4/22 from this website: http://cityofpraisechurch.com/wp-content/uploads/2021/08/LR-AUG-2021.pdf

2) Equip is defined this way in the Merriam-Webster online dictionary at this web link: http://www.merriam-webster.com/dictionary/equip

3) The World headline was taken from this website on 3/10/22 - https://theworld.org/stories/2019-05-30/ayatollah-khamenei-says-nuclear-weapons-are-forbidden-under-islamic-sharia-law

4) TOI quote taken from this website on 3/10/22 - https://www.timesofisrael.com/iran-general-says-tehran-aims-to-wipe-israel-off-the-political-map-report/

5) TOI quote taken from this website on 3/10/22 - https://www.timesofisrael.com/khamenei-when-iran-speaks-of-wiping-out-israel-it-refers-to-regime-not-jews/

6) TOI quote taken from this website on 3/10/22 - https://www.timesofisrael.com/iranian-commander-we-can-destroy-israel-in-under-8-minutes/

7) ABC headline was taken from this website on 3/11/22 - https://abcnews.go.com/International/wireStory/israel-readying-iran-conflict-officials-81078540

8) Reuters headline was taken from this website on 3/11/22 - https://www.reuters.com/article/iran-nuclear-gulf/gulf-countries-meet-over-iran-nuclear-radiation-fears-idUSL5N0D104K20130414

9) Wikipedia quote taken from this weblink: https://en.wikipedia.org/wiki/Nebuchadnezzar_II

10) Britannica quote taken from this website: https://www.britannica.com/biography/Nebuchadnezzar-II

11) Quote taken from this website: https://biblehub.com/commentaries/jeremiah/49-39.htm

12) Thompson quote taken from this website: https://www.livius.org/sources/content/mesopotamian-chronicles-content/abc-5-jerusalem-chronicle/

13) Elam timeline taken from this website on 8/22/22: https://www.scaruffi.com/politics/persians.html

14) Gaebelein quote taken from this website: https://www.studylight.org/commentaries/eng/gab/jeremiah-49.html

15) Walvoord quote taken from this website: https://christianarticles-blog.wordpress.com/2023/02/26/prophecies-of-elam/

16) TOI quote taken on 3/14/22 from this website: https://www.timesofisrael.com/idf-official-israel-expects-hezbollah-to-fire-2000-rockets-a-day-in-wartime/

17) Press TV quote taken on 3/14/22 from this website: https://www.presstv.ir/Detail/2019/05/13/595826/Israel-Gaza-Palestine-missile-power-Hezbollah-Hamas-Islamic-Jihad-Badr

18) NPR quote taken on 3/14/22 from this website: https://www.npr.org/2019/02/17/695545252/more-than-300-chemical-attacks-launched-during-syrian-civil-war-study-says

19) Reuters quote taken on 3/14/22 from this website: https://www.reuters.com/world/middle-east/israel-hit-chemical-weapons-facilities-syria-over-past-two-years-washington-post-2021-12-13/

20) National Interest quote taken on 3/14/22 from this website: https://nationalinterest.org/blog/buzz/israel-underwater-nuclear-power-thanks-german-submarines-57517

21) JP quote taken on 6/18/22 from this website: https://www.jpost.com/middle-east/article-709342

22) Reuters quote taken on 3/14/22 from this website: https://www.reuters.com/article/us-mideast-crisis-israel-syria-iran/israel-says-struck-iranian-targets-in-syria-200-times-in-last-two-years-idUSKCN1LK2D7

23) Olive tree quote taken from the Jerusalem Post at this website: https://www.jpost.com/israel-news/olive-tree-selected-as-israels-national-tree-by-kkl-jnf-657038

24) Nahal Sorek information taken from this website: https://en.wikipedia.org/wiki/Nahal_Sorek

25) JP headline taken on 6/21/22 from this website: https://www.jpost.com/israel-news/article-708466

26) UN Resolution 181 quote taken on 6/21/22 from this website: https://mfa.gov.il/Jubilee-years/Pages/1947-UN-General-Assembly-Resolution-181-The-international-community-says-Yes-to-the-establishment-of-the-State-of-Israel.aspx#:~:text=Resolution%20181%20was%20emphatically%20rejected,Jewish%20State%20by%20all%20means.

27) Jaramana image was taken on 6/23/22 from this website: https://margaridasantoslopes.com/1991/12/22/7665/)

28) Yashab interpretations taken from the NAS Exhaustive Concordance at this weblink: https://biblehub.com/hebrew/3427.htm

29) 300 of Gideon's men destroyed 120,000 Midianites, according to Judges 8:1-10.

30) Israel Today article was taken from this website: https://www.israel-today.co.il/read/psalm-83-and-israels-memorial-day/

31) JP article is from - https://www.jpost.com/israel-news/article-706226

32) Newsweek headline is from - https://www.newsweek.com/israel-simulate-massive-military-strike-iran-nuclear-fears-grow-1707532

33) TOI headline is from - https://www.timesofisrael.com/idf-drills-for-multi-front-war-including-1500-rockets-a-day-fired-from-lebanon/

34) Quote taken on 8/4/22 from this website: https://www.britannica.com/topic/United-Nations-Resolution-181

35) Zechariah 12 was likely written between 520-518 BC.

36) Wikipedia quote taken on 10/22/22 from this website link: https://en.wikipedia.org/wiki/Chariotry_in_ancient_Egypt#:~:text=Chariots%20were%20effective%20for%20their,from%20the%20tomb%20of%20Tutankhamun.

37) Parson's Technology Software, Quickverse Version 6.0, Barnes, Notes on the Old Testament, under "And the Hagarenes," (Austin, TX; n.d.).

38) Fruchtenbaum quote taken from his book, the Footsteps of the Messiah, page 506.

39) Author recommended books and / or articles, and / or videos presentations covering Ezekiel 38 are Northern Storm Rising by Dr. Ron Rhodes; Epicenter by Joel Rosenberg; The Magog Invasion and The Alternative View to the Magog Invasion by Dr. Chuck Missler; and The Footsteps of the Messiah by Dr. Arnold Fruchtenbaum.

40) Northern Storm Rising – Russia, Iran, And the Emerging End-Times Military Coalition Against Israel - Page 159 under "The Burial of Enemy Bodies for Seven Months (Ezekiel 39:11-12,14-16) Published by Harvest House - Copyright 2008. Authored by Dr. Ron Rhodes.

41) The Bible Knowledge Commentary: New Testament – commentary on the Fifth Trumpet.

42) Average lifespan of a locust was taken from this weblink: https://byjus.com/biology/locust-life-cycle/.

43) The Bible Knowledge Commentary: New Testament – commentary on the Sixth Trumpet.

44) (cf. Time, May 21, 1965, p. 35).

45) Reagan quote taken from this weblink: https://sermons.love/dr-david-r-reagan/10182-david-reagan-jesus-is-returning-soon-part-2.html.

46) Woods quote taken from 24 minute mark of this video link: https://www.youtube.com/watch?v=_6zERBmAP3Y.

47) Fruchtenbaum, The Footsteps of the Messiah, pg. 231.

48) Rhodes quote: The Popular Dictionary of Bible Prophecy by Ron Rhodes Harvest House Publishers 2010, page 9.

49) Congressional report taken from this weblink: https://sgp.fas.org/crs/row/R46808.pdf.

50) Mideast Population taken from this weblink: https://worldpopulationreview.com/continents/the-middle-east-population.

51) The Footsteps of the Messiah, A study of the sequence of Prophetic Events. Pg. 317.

52) The Footsteps of the Messiah, A study of the sequence of Prophetic Events. Pg. 507.

53) The Footsteps of the Messiah, A study of the sequence of Prophetic Events. Pg. 317-318.

54) Wikipedia quote taken from this weblink: https://en.wikipedia.org/wiki/Jezreel_Valley.

55) Talent weight taken from the Encyclopedia Britannica at this weblink: https://www.britannica.com/science/talent-unit-of-weight#ref181773.

56) Wiersbe's Expository outline on the New Testament.

57) Walvoord and Zuck: The Bible Knowledge Commentary: New Testament.

58) 9.0 results taken on 7/6/20 from this weblink: https://en.wikipedia.org/wiki/Richter_magnitude_scale.

59) 10.0 quote is from Prakash Jha, Scientist in Engineering Geophysics (1996-present), and was taken on 7/6/20 from this weblink: https://www.quora.com/How-would-an-earthquake-of-magnitude-10-on-the-Richter-scale-feel-like?no_redirect=1.

60) Mount Seir quote taken from this website on 5/30/23: https://en.wikipedia.org/wiki/Mount_Seir.

61) Arabia Petraea information was taken on 5/31/23 from these two weblinks: (1) https://en.wikipedia.org/wiki/Teman_(Edom)#:~:text=Teman%20(Hebrew%3A%20%D7%AA%D7%99%D7%9E%D7%9F)%2C,biblical%20town%20of%20Arabia%20

Petraea. (2) https://en.wikipedia.org/wiki/Arabia_Petraea.

62) Paran quote taken on 5/31/23 from this website: https://www.bible.ca/archeology/bible-archeology-exodus-route-wilderness-of-paran.htm.

63) Wilderness of Paran quote taken on 5/31/23 from this website: https://biblearchaeology.org/research/exodus-from-egypt/4012-What-Do-Mt-Horeb,-The-Mountain-of-God,-Mt-Paran-and-Mt-Seir-Have-to-Do-with-Mt-Sinai.

64) Paran quote taken from this website on 5/31/23: https://www.bibletools.org/index.cfm/fuseaction/Topical.show/RTD/cgg/ID/12424/Mount-Paran.htm.

65) National Geographic quote taken on 4/17/23 from this website: https://www.nationalgeographic.com/history/article/lost-city-petra

66) Petra Paths quote taken from this website on 5/30/23: https://www.engagingcultures.com/three-ways-to-enter-petra/#:~:text=Although%20the%20most%20popular%20way,%2DKhazneh%2C%20or%20the%20Treasury.

67) Bedouin quote taken from this website on 5/30/23: https://www.al-monitor.com/originals/2013/12/jordan-petra-cave-dwellers-neglect-authorities.html#:~:text=The%20Bedouins%20lived%20in%20the,city's%20caves%20and%20archaeological%20sites.

68) Petra water channels and pipeline quotes taken on 5/31/23 from this weblink: https://traveltalesoflife.com/petra-water-system/#:~:text=The%20Water%20Channels%20Petra,pipes%20that%20distributed%20the%20water.

69) The Footsteps of the Messiah, A study of the sequence of Prophetic Events. Pg. 361.

70) The Christian Post. 1 in 3 Americans Link Syrian Conflict to Bible's End-Time Prophecy Survey Finds September 14, 2013.

https://www.christianpost.com/news/1-in-3-americans-link-syrian-conflict-to-bibles-end-time-prophecy-survey-finds.html

71) Has The Destruction Of Damascus Been Fulfilled? March 5, 2019 https://jashow.org/articles/has-the-destruction-of-damascus-been-fulfilled/

72) The Middle East Meltdown video #29, 9/4/22 Andy Woods https://www.youtube.com/watch?v=TCYJ4WGmOAM&t=836s

73) The Middle East Meltdown video #28, 8/28/22 Andy Woods https://www.youtube.com/watch?v=sC2S6RKCKWU&t=614s

74) The Middle East Meltdown video #27, 8/21/22 Andy Woods
https://www.youtube.com/watch?v=p6ogURR3tag

75) The Middle East Meltdown video #29, 9/4/22 Andy Woods
https://www.youtube.com/watch?v=TCYJ4WGmOAM

76) The Middle East Meltdown video #29, 9/4/22 Andy Woods
https://www.youtube.com/watch?v=TCYJ4WGmOAM

77) The Middle East Meltdown video #29, 9/4/22 Andy Woods
https://www.youtube.com/watch?v=TCYJ4WGmOAM

78) Smith Bible Dictionary.
https://www.blueletterbible.org/search/Dictionary/viewTopic.cfm?topic=BT0001115

79) Easton's Bible Dictionary.
https://www.biblestudytools.com/dictionary/damascus/

80) Tyndale Bible Dictionary Philip Wesley Comfort, Walter A. Elwell Page 346 2001.

81) Ancient History from the Monuments: Assyria from Earliest Times to the Fall of Nineveh George Smith Pages 87-88.
https://www.google.com/books/edition/Ancient_History_from_the_Monuments/VS1PAAAAYAAJ?hl=en&gbpv=1&dq=george+smith+and+sixteen+districts+of+Damascus+were+destroyed+like+a+flood+..+591&pg=PA88&printsec=frontcover

82) Ellicott's Commentary for English Readers 1905.
https://biblehub.com/commentaries/ellicott/isaiah/17.htm

83) Annotated Bible Dr. Arno Gaebelein 1922.
https://truthaccordingtoscripture.com/commentaries/gab/isaiah-17.php#.YvZUSOjYpD8

84) Things To Come J. Dwight Pentecost 1958.
https://lionandlambapologetics.org/wp-content/uploads/2021/12/Things-to-Come-Pentecost.pdf

85) Every Prophecy of the Bible John F. Walvoord Pages 150-151 1999.

86) Jeremiah 49 - Words of Judgment Against The Nations Damascus Feinberg.
https://enduringword.com/bible-commentary/jeremiah-49/

87) Every Prophecy of the Bible John F. Walvoord Page 151 1999.

88) CONSISTENT BIBLICAL FUTURISM article Thomas Ice quoting Mark Hitchcock. https://www.pre-trib.org/pretribfiles/pdfs/Ice-ConsistentBiblicalFuturism_13.pdf

89) CONSISTENT BIBLICAL FUTURISM article Thomas Ice

https://www.pre-trib.org/pretribfiles/pdfs/Ice-ConsistentBiblicalFuturism_13.pdf

90) The Middle East Meltdown #30 Video 9/11/21

https://www.youtube.com/watch?v=J8yxBFVUVH0&t=163s

91) "Bill Salus, a True Eschatologist" by Dr. David Reagan in 2017.

http://www.prophecydepotministries.net/2017/bill-salus-the-star-trek-eschatologist-by-dr-david-reagan/

92) Believers Bible Commentary William McDonald pages 675-676 1995.

93) The Anchor Bible Psalms 51-100 Mitchell Dahood, S.J. page 273 1968.

94) The New American Commentary Psalms 73-150 Volume 13 Daniel J. Estes page 121-123 2019.

95) New Century Bible Psalms Volume 2 A.A. Anderson 595, 597, 600, 601 1972.

96) Lange Commentary on the Holy Scripture John Peter Lange

https://biblehub.com/commentaries/lange/psalms/83.htm

97) Lange Commentary on the Holy Scripture John Peter Lange

https://biblehub.com/commentaries/lange/psalms/83.htm